Four Views
on Christian Metaphysics

Four Views
on Christian Metaphysics

edited by
TIMOTHY M. MOSTELLER

CASCADE *Books* • Eugene, Oregon

FOUR VIEWS ON CHRISTIAN METAPHYSICS

Copyright © 2022 Wipf & Stock Publishers. All rights reserved. Except for brief quotations in critical publications or reviews, no part of this book may be reproduced in any manner without prior written permission from the publisher. Write: Permissions, Wipf and Stock Publishers, 199 W. 8th Ave., Suite 3, Eugene, OR 97401.

Cascade Books
An Imprint of Wipf and Stock Publishers
199 W. 8th Ave., Suite 3
Eugene, OR 97401

www.wipfandstock.com

PAPERBACK ISBN: 978-1-7252-7330-6
HARDCOVER ISBN: 978-1-7252-7331-3
EBOOK ISBN: 978-1-7252-7332-0

Cataloguing-in-Publication data:

Names: Mosteller, Timothy [editor] | Gould, Paul M., [author] | Jacobs, Timothy L. [author] | Spiegel, James S., [author] | Welbaum, Sam [author]

Title: Four views on Christian metaphysics / edited by Timothy M. Mosteller.

Description: Eugene, OR: Cascade Books, 2022 | Includes bibliographical references and index.

Identifiers: ISBN 978-1-7252-7330-6 (paperback) | ISBN 978-1-7252-7331-3 (hardcover) | ISBN 978-1-7252-7332-0 (ebook)

Subjects: LCSH: Metaphysics | Christianity—Philosophy | Philosophical theology | Platonists | Aristotle. Metaphysics | Idealism | Postmodernism

Classification: BT103 M67 2022 (paperback) | BT103 (ebook)

03/09/22

To Eddie Colanter, in friendship.

Contents

Introduction ix

Contributors xiii

1. Christian Metaphysics and Platonism — 1
2. Christian Metaphysics and Aristotelianism — 35
3. Christian Metaphysics and Idealism — 71
4. Christian Metaphysics and Postmodernism — 103

Index — 139

Introduction

Since the resurrection of Jesus and the completion of the New Testament, Christians have thought deeply about the nature of reality, what philosophers call metaphysics or ontology. Throughout the history of the Christian church, Christian philosophers have tried to offer a general metaphysics considering both biblical and general revelation. However, Christians have not always agreed on how to go about doing metaphysics. In addition, Christians differ on how to best answer some of the most fundamental questions in metaphysics, such as: What is the nature of existence itself? What is it for something to exist? What are universals? What is the soul? How does the nature of existence, things that do exist, universals and the soul relate to God, especially in light of special and general revelation? This book will present four prominent views held among Christians today on these questions in metaphysics.

There is a deep need in our culture, and especially in the church to be very clear about a Christian view of the nature of reality. We live in a deeply relativistic culture that takes reality to be simply dependent upon one's feelings or opinion. It is incumbent on Christian philosophers to be very clear as to how Christian leaders, teachers, and pastors should go about answering these deep questions. This book is intended to be useful for professional philosophers, students of philosophy (especially students in metaphysics courses), and scholars interested in the possible approaches to Christian metaphysics. It is our prayer that it will be helpful in the growth of your mind for the strengthening of your faith.

The four Christian perspectives presented in this book are: Platonism, Aristotelianism, idealism, and postmodernism. Each chapter author will answer several questions from their distinct perspective and reply to each of the other authors. The questions to be addressed are: What is metaphysics? How should metaphysics be done by Christians? What does Christian metaphysics tell us about: the nature of existence, universals, the human soul, and God's relation to them? In addition, at the end of each chapter, once each author has addressed the major areas of metaphysics from their perspective, they will summarize their position by addressing a case study of the resurrection so that the readers can see the key differences in each position.

SUMMARY OF THE FOUR VIEWS

Platonism as an approach to metaphysics is a form of dualistic realism. First, it maintains dualism. There are two parts to reality, physical and non-physical reality. Further, for Christian forms of Platonism, there is a dependency of the existence of physical reality on non-physical reality, specifically on God. Second, Platonism maintains realism. Both physical and non-physical reality are real, and independent from human cognition. There are different versions of Christian Platonism, but in general it will maintain that existence is found ultimately in God, that universals are real and related to God, that the soul has two parts (body and mind) and that all of these things are sustained in existence by God.

Aristotelianism shares with Platonic metaphysics aspects of its dualism and its realism. However, it maintains some distinctions from Platonism regarding the relation between the two parts of reality, physical and non-physical reality. For example, Aristotelians agree with Platonists that universals (like redness or humanity) are real, but they disagree as to whether these universals can exist uninstantiated (apart from the things that have them). Platonists will say yes, redness really exists even if there are no red things, while Aristotelians will deny this. Aristotelianism found its greatest champion in the history of Christian metaphysics in the person of Thomas Aquinas. Christian Aristotelians often follow Aquinas' lead in making sense of the nature of existence, the nature of the soul (again a form of dualism, but very different from that of Platonism), and the nature of universals, especially as to their relation to the mind of God.

Idealism is very distinct from both Platonism and Aristotelianism in that it is (like materialism) distinctively *not dualistic*. Idealism is a form of monism. There is only one kind of substance, not two. While there are a variety of "idealisms" in the history of metaphysics, the most prominent form was defended by George Berkeley. Berkeleyan idealism maintains that all of physical reality is a collection of ideas, and what we take to be different types of physical bodies (books, chairs, shoes, etc.) are really all ideas. Idealism maintains a very strong role for God in Christian metaphysics, since it is claimed that "to be is to be perceived." That is, everything that is real is real because of God's perception of it. Idealism of this form will give an account of how all of reality is *ideal* in nature and how it is dependent upon the mind of God.

Postmodernism is a more recent approach to metaphysics than either the dualistic realism of Platonism and Aristotelianism or the monism of idealism. Postmodernism can be broadly characterized as a marked shift in how metaphysics was understood up through "modernity." It generally rejects metaphysics as an "analysis" of "reality" but rather sees the project of metaphysics as a broadly hermeneutical or interpretive task that rejects grand-scale systems. For example, it often rejects the realism of both Platonism and Aristotelianism in favor of a nominalist view of universals. Universals are simply names *we agree upon* in our use of language. Christian post-modernism may approach metaphysics as a personal, spiritual, phenomenological task that incorporates the contingent aspects of lived reality as seen through the interpretive lenses of contingent creatures, but while connecting lived experience to the God of the Bible.

A MATERIALIST LACUNA: EDITOR'S APOLOGY

In editing any book on any subject, one must choose what gets included and what excluded. As a student of philosophy, you are likely familiar with metaphysical materialism. It is a view that, in my opinion, is the default position of many in the academy who reject all four of the views considered in this volume, but who are not themselves relativists about the nature of reality. It may be a dominant view in the natural sciences, or among what has been called the "new atheist" movement. It is a view that is crassly, and popularly put forward by Bertrand Russell in his essay, *A Free Man's Worship*.

There may be varieties of materialism as broad approaches to metaphysics, and there may be philosophers (both Christian and otherwise) who are selectively materialists in portions of their ontologies (e.g. materialists about the human person). Materialism as a broad approach to metaphysics shares with idealism a monistic tendency. It will agree with idealism, that there is only one kind of thing, but it will claim that the one kind of thing that exists is not *mental*, rather the one kind of thing that exists is *material*. The details of what exactly "material" amounts to, will vary according to the opinion of various materialist philosophers. It is probably safe to say that materialism is a monistic view of the nature of all reality, which is captured best in the categories of the discipline of physics (whether present or future). Thus characterized, materialism will disagree with dualism, both Platonism and Aristotelianism. While some forms of materialism might be compatible with post-modernism broadly speaking, it is my opinion that complete across-the-board metaphysical materialism is simply incompatible with the Christian faith.

One might show that metaphysical materialism is incompatible with Christian faith by focusing on the main object of the Christian faith, which is the God of the Bible. Christians have generally thought that we can know God from both natural reason in the natural world *and* through revelation from God in the Scriptures. While the claim that God can be known (and how) by natural means is a perennial debate among Christian philosophers, there is still much to be said in favor of knowing God from natural evidence. It seems to me that one of the stronger cases to be made for the God of the Bible available today is a cumulative-case argument that has as its central conclusion that there exists an immaterial personal being who cares about the universe, and who is the immaterial being upon whom the physical cosmos depends for its existence. Such a view has been developed by Christian philosophers such as William Lane Craig, J. P. Moreland, and Dallas Willard among others. If these views are right, then wholesale metaphysical materialism cannot also be true. The two are simply incompatible. In addition, in Christian revelation, we have the words of Jesus in John 4:24, "God is Spirit." While this is not the place for a lengthy word study of the Greek term "pneuma," the plain reading of this text is that God is certainly not material. This seems to be the view of the Hebrew Scriptures, Jesus himself, as well as the church throughout its history. If this is correct, then broad metaphysical materialism is also incompatible with Christian revelation.

Having said this, it is possible for a Christian to try to maintain their commitment to the nature of God as immaterial from both reason and revelation, *and* try to maintain some form of partial or limited ontological materialism, say for example about human nature, the nature of the human soul, the nature of universals, free will, or even created existence apart from God. However, since this book is a comparison of *complete* metaphysics (metaphysics in the broad sense of *being qua being*) and its application to both God and created reality, it seemed to me best to limit the discussion to four views that are at least plausibly compatible with what we know about God from reason and revelation. This is not to say that different varieties of limited Christian materialism are not worthy of consideration or careful study, nor is it to say that there is not a need for good books on the topics of most interest to Christian materialist thinkers and their debates with other views. This will especially be the case for a *Christian* materialism with regard to what it means to be human and the human soul. Whether or not any version of Christian materialism, whether partial or total, can be successfully defended remains to be seen, but it will not be considered directly in this volume. What is considered here are four Christian views of metaphysics. Whether any of them are successful, either in part or whole, or in some combination, is left to the judgment of the reader.

Contributors

Paul M. Gould (PhD, Purdue University) is associate professor of philosophy of religion and director of the M.A. Philosophy of Religion program at Palm Beach Atlantic University. He has published eleven books, including *Beyond the Control of God? Six Views on the Problem of God and Abstract Objects* (Bloomsbury), *Cultural Apologetics* (Zondervan), and *Philosophy: A Christian Introduction* with Jamie Dew (Baker). He has been a visiting scholar at Trinity Evangelical Divinity School's Henry Center, working on the intersection of science and faith, and is the founder and president of the Two Tasks Institute. You can find out more about him and his work at www.paul-gould.com and https://www.twotasksinstitute.org. He is married to Ethel and has four children, all of whom roll their eyes when he starts to wax philosophical around the dinner table. He likes to hike with his family, exploring God's handiwork and seeing how all things point to and illuminate the divine.

Timothy L. Jacobs (Teaching Fellow, The Davenant Institute, and PhD candidate, University of St. Thomas, Houston) has taught at the University of St. Thomas, Lone Star College, and Houston Community College. He has written for *Lexham Bible Dictionary* (Lexham Press, 2014), the *Jonathan Edwards Encyclopedia* (Yale University Press, 2017), as well as a couple dozen articles, some of which may be viewed at www.tljacobs.com. His interests are in virtue, natural law, Aristotle, Aquinas, classical logic, and classical theism. His research aims to help Protestantism be more historically rooted in classical thought, as the Reformers were. He also teaches philosophy and apologetics at church. His love of realist metaphysics has partially come from his longtime hobby of discussing philosophy and subcreation in fantasy literature, role playing games, and movies with his wife and friends.

James S. Spiegel (Ph.D. Michigan State University) is a professional philosopher and expert in the philosophy of George Berkeley and idealism.

He has taught a range of courses in philosophy, and authored or edited eleven books and more than ninety articles on issues in ethics, aesthetics, philosophy of religion, and popular culture, including *The Benefits of Providence* (Crossway), the two-volume Idealism and Christianity series (Bloomsbury), and the award-winning *How to Be Good in a World Gone Bad* (Kregel). In addition to teaching and writing, Jim speaks regularly at professional conferences, colleges, and churches and is often interviewed for podcasts and radio programs. For ideal fun, he enjoys song-writing and music production.

Sam Welbaum (PhD, Claremont Graduate University) is assistant professor of philosophy, and the director of the Honors Program, at California Baptist University. He has also taught at Colorado Christian University, Gateway Seminary, has served as both a youth pastor and associate pastor, and was a host of the Apologetics.com Radio Show. He has published and presented papers in the areas of aesthetics, social philosophy, miracles, worldview, and the philosophy of humor. His current research interests are the relationship between boredom, secularism, and modernity; nostalgia; and the relationship between worship and catharsis. For fun Sam likes to play board games, go on adventures with his family (often to aquariums), dabble in astronomy, and re-watch culturally significant TV shows to see how they have influenced our understanding of the world. He is also thankful for the metaphysical reality of chicken wings and bbq sauce.

1

Christian Metaphysics and Platonism

1.1 Platonism—Paul M. Gould
1.2 Aristotelianism Response—Timothy L. Jacobs
1.3 Idealism Response—James S. Spiegel
1.4 Postmodernism Response—Sam Welbaum
1.5 Platonism Reply—Paul M. Gould

1.1 PLATONISM—PAUL M. GOULD

Taxonomy of Platonisms

In this essay, I develop and defend a Christian Platonic metaphysic as the best overall metaphysical theory. Since there are many versions of Platonism, it will be helpful to provide a taxonomy of Platonisms in order to properly locate my proposal.

First, there is *traditional Platonism*. This is the Platonism of eternal forms, immortal souls, and the diminution of the material world.[1] The eternal and unchanging intelligible realm is more real than the temporal and changing sensible realm. Eternal souls are imprisoned in (evil) material bodies during each iteration on earth and seek release, and thus purification, upon death. This is the version of Platonism that is regularly and rightly criticized by Christian theologians, especially because of its gnostic denigration of the material world, as unbiblical. I am not defending a version of traditional Platonism.

---

1. Smith, "Will the Real Plato Please Stand Up?" 64.

Second, there is *contemporary Platonism*. In the medieval period, the debate over Platonism centered on the problem of universals.[2] The Platonist or realist argued that there are universals whereas the nominalist argued that there are no universals. The realist believed in Plato's world of eternal forms, the nominalist didn't. The debate over Platonism shifted in the nineteenth and twentieth centuries away from a debate regarding universals to a debate about abstract objects. The contemporary Platonist thinks abstract objects exist. The contemporary nominalist denies their existence. While it is notoriously difficult to give a precise definition of "abstract object," it is generally agreed to be immaterial, nonspatial, necessary (setting aside sets with contingent members), and eternal (again, setting aside sets and perhaps fictional objects) non-agents. While abstract objects are typically thought to be causally impotent, I allow that they can enter into causal relations and that some (i.e., concepts/divine ideas) play a *formal* causal role in divine creation. Unless noted otherwise, I shall understand abstract objects as described. I think the debate over universals and the debate over abstract objects overlap, and will address this overlap below.[3]

Finally, there is *contemporary Christian Platonism* (CCP). The contemporary Christian Platonist affirms the existence of, among other things, the Triune God and abstract objects. There are many versions of CCP. I shall defend a version that endorses the following two *theological* principles:

> AD: (i) God does not depend on anything distinct from himself for his existing, and (ii) everything distinct from God depends on God for its existing.
>
> SU: God is (i) the creator and sustainer of the universe, and (ii) ontologically distinct from the universe yet present and active in the universe. (iii) The universe points beyond itself to the sacred order.[4]

---

2. For a helpful summary of the two debates over Platonism, see Rodriquez-Pereyra, "Nominalism in Metaphysics."

3. As James K. A. Smith points out, in the battle over gnostic escapism, Plato is understandably seen as the enemy of traditional Christian theology. But when it comes to the battle with naturalistic materialism, along with its reductionistic and scientistic tendencies, Platonism becomes a powerful antidote and friend of Christian theism. I aim to exploit this more theistic friendly side of Platonism. See Smith, "Will the Real Plato Please Stand Up?" 62 footnote 1.

4. Biblical support for *AD* and clause (i) and (ii) of SU include Genesis 1:1; Exodus 3:14; John 1:3; Acts 17:28; Romans 11:36; Ephesians 3:9; Colossians 1:15–20; and Revelation 4:11. Biblical support for clause (iii) of *SU* include Job 12:7–9; Psalm 19:1–2; Matthew 6:28–30; and Romans 1:19–20; 2:15.

God exists and the world exists. The "world" refers to any existent reality, material or immaterial, that is distinct from God. So, there is God and the world. As the sole ultimate reality, God exists *a se*, everything distinct from God depends on God. The aseity-sovereignty doctrine *AD* preserves God's ultimacy. My commitment to *AD* distinguishes my version of *CCP* from those developed by *inter alia* Keith Yandell, Peter van Inwagen, and Nicholas Wolterstorff who posit independently existing abstract objects.[5]

My commitment to a "sacramental universe" (*SU*) requires some unpacking.[6] The "universe" refers to the material cosmos, the "one gigantic spatio-temporal whole" composed of (in ascending order) fundamental particles, molecules, medium-sized objects, planets, stars, and galaxies.[7] I am not claiming that the universe is *wholly* material, but it is not less than material. There is more to "the world" than the universe, however. There are nonmaterial realities, including souls, angels, and abstract objects. These nonmaterial realities are part of the world, and hook up to the universe in diverse ways, to be explained in this essay. Clauses (i) and (ii) of *SU* are intended to preserve a robust doctrine of divine transcendence and immanence that affirms the createdness, goodness, materiality, integrity, and grace-infused nature of the universe. Of course, much hangs on how God is understood to be present and active "in" the universe. I'll develop a participatory ontology that upholds the creator/creature distinction and insists, following Aquinas, that "God be in all things, and intimately so."[8] On *SU*, God is not identical to the world (i.e., pantheism) nor is the world a part of God (i.e., panentheism). God and the world are ontologically distinct yet tightly bound together. Clause (iii) of *SU* specifies one of the functions the physical universe plays in the divine economy. The universe functions *semiotically*, as a sign that points beyond itself to the sacred order.[9] I shall understand "the sacred order" as *the realm of God and the enacted plan of God to create, sustain, and redeem the universe in Christ*. According to *SU*, the universe God has made can only be fully known when an account is

---

5. See Yandell, "God and Propositions," 21–35, 46–50; van Inwagen, "God and Other Uncreated Things," 3–20; and Wolterstorff, *On Universals*, chapter 12.

6. The term "sacramental universe" was first used in the modern era by William Temple in Temple, *Nature, Man and God*.

7. Grossmann, *The Existence of the World*, 8.

8. Aquinas, *Summa Theologiae*, 1.8.1.

9. The semiotic function of the cosmos was a commonly held view for those theologians belonging to what Hans Boersma calls "The Great Tradition" of Christian thought. The Great Tradition refers to the Platonic-Aristotelian-Christian synthesis held in common for "most of the Christian era until the late Middle Ages," Boersma *Heavenly Participation*, 20. See also Taylor, *A Secular Age*, 25–26.

given of the God-world relationship, a relationship that specifies God's involvement with all creation.

My version of *CCP* aims to provide an account of the God-world relationship that preserves *AD* and *SU* as well as the goodness and integrity of all created reality, including material reality and creaturely causes. It's time to describe my view. I argue for a modified Platonism called modified theistic activism (*MTA*).[10] Thomas Morris and Christopher Menzel are leading defenders of a version of *CCP* called theistic activism (*TA*). Morris and Menzel identify all abstract objects, including properties and relations, with constituents in the divine mind. My *MTA* is a *modified* theistic activism; I do not identify all abstracta with constituents of the divine mind. *MTA* and *TA* do share the conviction, however, that everything distinct from God is created by God. According to *MTA*, abstract objects exist. Some abstract objects exist as constituents of the divine substance. God has properties and stands in various relations to his ideas and thoughts. Regarding God's essential properties, they exist as uncreated constituents of the divine substance. Other properties, those that are not part of or essential to God, exist in a distinct realm—call it Plato's heaven, call it the abstract realm, or whatever. The created properties and relations reside in this realm. So, regarding properties and relations, some exist as uncreated constituents within God and the rest exist distinct from and created by God. According to *MTA*, concepts are identified with divine ideas and propositions with divine thoughts. Thinking is a productive activity and so, in thinking, God is the creator of concepts (i.e., divine ideas) and propositions (i.e., divine thoughts). This view regarding concepts and propositions is endorsed by Alvin Plantinga, Thomas Morris, and Christopher Menzel.[11] In sum: there are abstract objects in God and some in a distinct realm. Regarding those abstract objects that are proper parts or constituents of the divine substance, some exist as uncreated constituents (i.e., God's essential properties) and others as created constituents, either via an act of the divine will (in the case of God's non-essential properties) or an act of divine thinking. Those abstract objects that exist distinct from God are created by God via an act of the divine will (more below).[12]

---

10. I defend *MTA*, along with Richard Brian Davis, in Gould and Davis, *Beyond the Control of God*, 51–64, 75–79.

11. Plantinga, "Augustinian Christian Philosophy" 291–320; Morris and Menzel, "Absolute Creation," 352–62.

12. Due to space limitations, I set aside discussion of numbers, sets, possible worlds, and states of affairs. Each of these objects are derivative abstract objects "built-up" out of properties, meanings, substances, or some combination of them. For more on numbers and sets, see especially Menzel, "Theism, Platonism, and the Metaphysics of Mathematics."

With a taxonomy of Platonisms in place and the view I wish to defend stated, I now turn to the question of methodology in metaphysics. I will state what I take to be the central tasks and corresponding methodology the Christian metaphysician ought to adopt and show how this methodology naturally leads to a Christian Platonic metaphysics in general, and *MTA* in particular, as the best overall metaphysical account of reality.

Toward a Platonic Methodology in Metaphysics

Metaphysics studies the nature and structure of reality. The *Christian* metaphysician seeks an account of the nature and structure of reality that is faithful to Scripture. The Bible is not primarily a work of metaphysics, but it does make important metaphysical claims. To wit, we learn from Scripture about ultimate reality, God, the world, and divine action in the world. It is widely recognized that these truths are under-determined in Scripture. In other words, while Scripture teaches, e.g., that God is almighty or wholly good, it is the job of the philosopher to precisely define these divine attributes. The same goes for the biblical teaching regarding the material world, humans, and divine action in the world. The Bible functions, as Thomas Morris describes, as a "control" over philosophical theorizing.[13] But given the open texture of the biblical revelation, there is considerable freedom (and work) to be done by the Christian metaphysician in order to bring the truths of Scripture into coherence with the deliverance of empirical evidence from science and plausible accounts of reality from metaphysics.

I don't think there are any knock-down arguments, short of demonstrating logical incoherence, that definitively show one mature metaphysical theory as *the* one true theory. Rather, in metaphysics, like philosophy in general, there are always a number of views that could be true. Thus, the goal in metaphysics is to argue for the rational superiority of one's account in terms of certain theoretical virtues, virtues typically thought to be truth-indicative. Chief among the theoretical virtues are explanatory scope, explanatory power, and simplicity or elegance. Alas, it is rare that any theory will lay claim to all the theoretical virtues. In theory assessment, there will always be a weighing of benefits with costs in the search for a rationally superior mature theory. In what follows, I shall argue that *MTA* is the rationally superior metaphysic for the Christian because it is consistent with the deliverances of Scripture, including AD and *SU*, and it has what I think are the most important theoretical virtues (explanatory scope and power, empirical adequacy)

---

13. Morris, *Anselmian Explorations*, 25. The context of Morris' discussion is perfect being theology, but his point applies equally to the deliverances of Scripture.

even though it is a at times unlovely (i.e., it isn't a simple theory, although this isn't much of a cost since reality isn't simple either).

With the nature of Christian metaphysics now stated, how ought we conceive our tasks and method? I now state and briefly defend in a step-wise manner the claim that the proper methodology for the Christian metaphysician is a Platonic methodology. In other words, given AD and SU, our proper starting point in metaphysics is the spiritual realm, the realm of Plato's gods, and not the sensible realm, the realm of Plato's giants.[14]

Much of contemporary analytic philosophy, including philosophy of religion, conceives its primary tasks and methodology in Quinean terms: identify the best theory of the world and a canonical logic, translate the one into the other, specify the domain of quantification, and then inventory the domain of quantification without overlap and redundancy. For the Quinean, any variable that finds itself within the bounds of the existential quantifier in a properly formed sentence of first-order logic refers to a genuine entity, a piece of furniture in the world. Everything else is eliminated. The Quinean is not concerned with how reality fits together or whether one entity depends upon another. Reality is *flat*. The only relevant question, for any alleged object *o*, is whether or not it belongs to the set of existents.

The Christian metaphysician ought to reject the Quinean conception of metaphysics. As Jonathan Schaffer has pointed out, existence questions are relatively trivial whereas the question of fundamentality is interesting and illuminating. Moreover, the Quinean task and methodology can't be carried out until questions of fundamentality are addressed.[15] The question of fundamentality has to do with the notion of metaphysical dependency; the question of what grounds what. While existence questions are intertwined with questions of fundamentality, it is the question of fundamentality that ought to be central in metaphysics, since fundamentality more deeply reveals the nature and structure of reality.

For the Christian metaphysician committed to AD and SU, there are additional reasons for rejecting the Quinean conception. For given AD, the concept of "metaphysical priority" is already nonempty: God is the ungrounded ground of all distinct reality. Thus, *metaphysical foundationalism*, the view that God is the metaphysical foundation to all reality, is true. And given SU, God is the originating cause of the universe's existence and the sustaining cause of the universe's persistence. Regarding God's status as

---

14. In the *Sophist*, Plato describes a battle over the nature of reality between the giants, who "[drag] everything down to earth from the heavenly region" and the gods who "insist violently that true being is certain nonbodily forms that can be thought about," Plato, *Sophist*, 246a-c, 267—68.

15 See Schaffer "On What Grounds What."

creator, we might ask then, what did God create when he created the universe? A reasonable answer, following a version of Occam's razor such that one ought not to multiply *fundamental* entities beyond what is necessary, all that God would need to create are the fundamentals. Schaffer calls this version of the razor the "bang for the buck" principle: the best metaphysical theory is the one that generates the most derivative entities from the sparsest base of fundamentals.[16] Since fundamentality is a degreed concept, we can distinguish between absolute fundamentality and relative fundamentality. On the God-world scale, God is absolutely fundamental, all else is derivative. But when it comes to the world God has made, it is still possible to talk in terms of fundamental beings, now understood as fundamental relative to the created realm. In creating the (relative) fundamentals, God creates the world. This suggests the following broadly Aristotelian task and method:

T1: The task of metaphysics is to identify the fundamentals.

This task is accomplished by employing what Schaffer calls "diagnostics."[17] The idea is that we specify criteria for a metaphysical theory and then employ those criteria as guides in theory construction. These criteria would include at least *completeness* such that the fundamentals "cover" the world without overlap or gap, as well as *generality*, such that the fundamentals ground all metaphysical possibilities.[18] I specify a corresponding method as follows:

M1: Deploy diagnostics for what is fundamental.

But task T1 can't be our only task, for at least three reasons. First, given *AD*, there is metaphysical structure to reality due to the God-world relation (i.e., the world metaphysically depends upon God). Reality is not, contra Quine, flat. Second, as suggested above, given *SU* and the fact that God creates the fundamentals in creating the universe, there is metaphysical structure *within* the universe (i.e., the universe is ordered with respect to metaphysical priority and posteriority via well-founded grounding chains between fundamental and derivative entities). Third, given *SU*, God creates and sustains the universe according to a plan. There is an ordering and directing to the universe, including cosmic history. These considerations suggest the following additional task for the Christian metaphysician:

---

16. Schaffer "On What Grounds What," 361.
17. Schaffer "On What Grounds What," 351.
18. For a discussion of these diagnostics, as well as some others that Schaffer employs in his own neo-Aristotelian account of methodology in metaphysics, see Schaffer "On What Grounds What," 377–78.

> T2: The task of metaphysics is to identify *how* the fundamentals fit into a comprehensive whole directed toward an end.

How should we accomplish task T2? What principle or set of principles should we deploy to explain the unity and diversity we find in the universe? It is not difficult to see, given a commitment to *AD* and *SU*, that a Christian metaphysic is an instance of what Lloyd Gerson calls top-downism.[19] The idea is that the explanatory principles for any metaphysical theory about reality are derived from the spiritual or intelligible or divine realm. But then it follows that a Christian methodology in metaphysics ought to be a top-down methodology too. But top-downism is a central feature, as Gerson notes, of Platonism. Thus, the methodology I suggest, as an instance of top-downism, is a broadly Platonic methodology:

> M2: Deploy first-principles derivable from the sacred order to explain how the fundamentals fit together into a comprehensive whole directed toward an end.

Thus, a Platonic methodology in metaphysics seeks to identify the fundamentals (task T1) and to identify how they fit together (task T2) according to first-principle derivable from ultimate reality.

There is one more task suggested by *SU*, and this final task makes the need for a Platonic methodology explicit. *SU* reminds us that nature and the natural are never wholly autonomous nor wholly physical. In some sense, the universe participates in the divine (and vice-versa). This suggests one final task for the Christian metaphysician committed to *AD* and *SU*:

> T3: The task of metaphysics is to identify how the creaturely fundamentals *participate* in the absolute fundamental being (i.e., God).

Task T3 is inclusive of T1 and T2, serving to pull tightly together the sacred and natural orders. Specifying how the created order participates in God's being or goodness or love helps elucidate the sacredness of a universe created by God. How might task T3 be accomplished? Following Plato and the Platonic tradition, I begin by noting that the participation relation was called upon to play certain roles in a mature metaphysical theory. For example, Plato called upon the notion of participation to account for the *character* of things and Plotinus called upon the notion of participation to account for the *character* and *existence* of things.[20] As the primary relation

---

19. Gerson, *Aristotle and Other Platonists*, 32.
20. Schindler, "What's the Difference? On the Metaphysics of Participation in a Christian Context," 10.

that joins together God and finite substances (i.e., concrete reality), the Christian Platonist will aim to elucidate via the participation relation the way God *gifts being* to numerically distinct (from God) creatures. This suggest the following methodology for accomplishing task T3:

> M3: Identify the role(s) the participation relation plays in a theory and provide an account of participation consistent with the fundamental ontology identified by methods M1 and M2.

With my broadly Platonic tasks and methodology now stated, I now turn to my prescribed tasks in order to develop and (briefly) defend *MTA*.

The Fundamentals

Our first task is to identify the fundamentals. Guided by *completeness* and *generality*, I now argue that God creates, in creating the world, three fundamental entities: *substances*, *properties*, and *meanings* (i.e., concepts and propositions). God's creative act is sovereign, rational, and free. There are three *logical moments* of divine creative activity.[21] In the first logical moment (called the Biggest Bang, following Brian Leftow) God creates *possibilia*.[22] This moment is spontaneous and free and a movement of the divine intellect where God dreams up all creaturely possibilities. In this creative moment, all modal reality is set: concepts (and possible individuals) are divine ideas; propositions (and possible worlds) are divine thoughts.[23] The relation between a thought and a thinker is a *productive* relation;[24] God *creates* concepts and propositions via divine intellectual activity. In the second logical moment (called the Bigger Bang) God creates the *abstracta* that populate the Platonic realm. This moment is a necessary consequence of the first logical moment: God creates, of necessity and in virtue of the divine will, the Platonic horde of monadic and polyadic properties (i.e., relations) that play the role of structure making in any actual physical universe. In the third logical moment (the Big Bang) God creates the physical universe, i.e., *concreta*. This moment is deliberate and free and via the divine will. God's

---

21. For a full explication and defense of the activist account of divine creative activity, see Gould, "Theistic Activism and the Doctrine of Creation."

22. Brian Leftow, *God and Necessity*, 272–98.

23. This activist model of divine creative activity is not a full-blown deity theory, where the content of the divine nature *determines* what God thinks up in the Biggest Bang. Some modal reality is grounded in the divine nature and some (including creaturely essences and I-facts) is grounded in God's free and spontaneous intellectual activity.

24. Alvin Plantinga, *Where the Conflict Really Lies*, 291.

single creative act is complex: there is one logical moment that is necessary (the middle bang), one that is spontaneous and free (the first bang), and one that is deliberate and free (the third bang). In creating the fundamentals, God's creative activity "covers" the world without overlap or gap and accounts for all metaphysical possibilities. Beginning with the universe and the Big Bang and then working backwards, I now provide an account and (brief) defense of the fundamentals.

Substance. When God created the universe, what did God make? The answer: substances. Substances are the fundamental *concrete, material* objects that cover the universe without overlap or gap. The "universe" just is the sum of concrete material substances. I am not claiming that substances are *wholly* material. All substances have abstract objects as constituents and for at least some—e.g., humans—substances are body-soul composites. Still, given the deep unity of substances, it is appropriate to label the substances that constitute the "universe" as *material* substances, even though they are not wholly material.

I adopt a substance-attribute framework, whole-part priority, and causal pluralism to explicate my broadly Aristotelian theory of substance.[25] A substance can be defined as a fundamental unity of parts, properties, and powers ordered for the sake of the entity's proper functioning. As a fundamental unity, the substance is the ground, its parts, property instances, and its powers are the grounded. The direction of metaphysical and mereological grounding is from the whole to its parts: a substance's parts, property instances, and powers are non-separable parts of the whole, where x is a non-separable part of y if x's existence and identity is grounded in and dependent upon y.[26] I distinguish between a substance's nature (or substantial form) and its essential and accidental properties. I further distinguish between two kinds of properties: categorical (i.e., qualitative) and dispositional (i.e., powers). Substances *are* particularized natures and they *have* properties. A substance's properties flow from and are grounded in its nature. I side with the real essentialist, defining a thing's nature in non-modal terms, instead of the modal essentialist, who defines a thing's nature in terms of its essential properties. Natures function teleologically, determining the properties, powers, and integral parts had by the substance and directing these

---

25. For a more detailed account and defense of my understanding of substances, see Gould, "Neo-Aristotelian Accounts of Divine Creation," and Gould and Davis, "Where the Bootstrapping Really Lies: A Neo-Aristotelian Reply to Panchuk."

26. My account of substance is a version of *hylomorphism*; substances are form-matter composites, where "matter" is defined relationally as any non-separable aspect, property instance, or power of the substantial whole.

(metaphysical and physical) parts toward the entity's proper functioning, and in the case of animate substances, the entity's flourishing.

Property. As noted, substances are thickly characterized objects. In addition to characterized objects, I endorse *characters*, i.e., properties. Properties play a structure-making role in the universe, partially explaining the character of characterized objects. My case for properties begins by noting that there is *distinctiveness* and *unity* in the universe. There are qualitative facts (i.e., "a is F," "a is G") and resemblance facts (i.e., "a and b are both F") that cry out for explanation. I've defended elsewhere that universals, understood as shareable properties, offers the best explanation for these facts, both in terms of ideological economy (less primitives than the ostrich nominalist, the reductive nominalist, and the trope nominalist) and, perhaps surprisingly, in terms of *qualitative* ontological economy (the realist posits less fundamental *kinds* of things than the ostrich nominalist, the reductive nominalist, and the trope nominalist).[27]

Properties exist and many of them are shareable (i.e., universals). I further argue that universals (and properties in general) are transcendent abstract objects. The *immanent realist* thinks universals are wholly located at distinct places at once whereas the *Platonic realist* thinks that universals are multiply instantiated without being located at a place. I accept what Reinhardt Grossmann calls the "axiom of localization" such that "no entity whatsoever can exist at different places at once or at interrupted time intervals."[28] Rejecting the axiom of localization leads to absurd consequences. For example, in juggling two red balls, the immanent realist is committed to the bizarre claim that the universal *redness*, instantiated in two numerically distinct balls, is both moving away and toward itself when juggled. It is better to hold that abstract objects (i.e., properties) are nonspatially "in" concrete objects as metaphysical parts or constituents.

I distinguish between properties and property instances. Properties are simple, non-spatially located abstract objects whereas property instances are complex, concrete objects constituted by a particular (e.g., a substance, an integral part of a substance, or a bare particular), a property, and the exemplification relation (also a non-spatial object).[29] I adopt an abundant theory of properties in this sense: any meaningful predicate, setting aside predicates that lead to Russellian paradox, refers to a property. The

---

27. See Gould "There Are Universals." See also Gould "Properties and Universals."

28. Grossmann, *The Existence of the World*, 13.

29. Thus, I side with the constituent ontologist when it comes to accounting for how substances have properties. For a nice defense of a version of Platonist constituent ontology I find attractive, see Moreland, "Exemplification and Constituent Realism."

properties that God creates exist in a transcendent realm, Plato's heaven, and are either exemplified, unexemplified, or unexemplifiable.

Meanings. I use the term "meanings" to denote any essentially intentional objects in a comprehensive metaphysical theory. I posit two essentially intentional fundamental objects: concepts and propositions. Concepts *mediate* between the mind and the world; propositions *represent* the world as being a certain way and can be true or false.[30] My claim is not that concepts and propositions are the only intentional objects in a comprehensive theory, for linguistic entities such as words and sentences can possess *derivative* intentionality. Rather, the claim is that they are the only kind of fundamental objects that have intentional properties essentially. But how, we might ask, can concepts and propositions be essentially intentional? I side with those who think the notion of mind-independent essentially intentional objects is at least fantastical if not unintelligible.[31] Rather, essential intentionality is the mark of the mental.[32] It is reasonable then to think that concepts and propositions, as mental objects, are ideas and thoughts. But whose ideas and thoughts? Arguably, given the scarcity and fragility of human ideas and thoughts, it is best to identify concepts and propositions with *divine* ideas and *divine* thoughts.[33]

I use the terms "concept" and "proposition" when referring to meanings relative to the world. In the act of thinking, *humans* have concepts and entertain propositions. Concepts and propositions are shareable and repeatable and thus objective in the sense that they exist independently of the (finite) subjects who have them. Concepts and propositions are universals and (as discussed above) since universals are abstract objects, concepts and propositions are abstract objects too. The claim that concepts and propositions are abstract is in apparent tension with the claim that concepts are divine ideas and propositions are divine thoughts. For ideas and thoughts are paradigm particulars and particulars are *concrete* objects. Consider my thought (T) *The thought that Plantinga is wise.* (T) is a mental token,

---

30. In our defense of *MTA* (Gould and Davis, "Modified Theistic Activism"), we argue that if propositions are complex wholes then they are best thought of as divine thoughts. For an argument that propositions are divine thoughts that remains neutral with respect to the ontological structure of propositions (i.e., complex or simple), see Keller, "The Argument from Intentionality (or Aboutness)."

31. For the claim that positing intentional-but-nonmental objects is fantastical, see Plantinga, *Where the Conflict Really Lies,* 288; and for the claim that it is unintelligible, see Jubien, "Propositions and the Objects of Thought," 53–54.

32. Crane, "Intentionality as the Mark of the Mental," 229–51.

33. For arguments from essentially intentional objects to God, in addition to Keller's "The Argument from Intentionality (or Aboutness)," see also Anderson and Welty, "The Lord of Noncontradiction: An Argument for God from Logic."

a grasping of the proposition (P) *Plantinga is wise*. There is a distinction between the token (T) and the type (P). My thought (T) is only derivatively intentional; proposition (P) is the essentially intentional object that grounds my thought's intentionality. In the divine case, however, there is no distinction between thought and proposition. *Ex hypothesi*, God's thought *is* the proposition; God's thought is essentially intentional. So, regarding the abstract vs. concrete question, we have a choice to make. On the one hand, divine ideas and thoughts are particular since they're specific ideas and thoughts God has. On the other hand, they're universal in that many (finite) particulars might grasp or instantiate them. We can either pull apart concrete and particular and argue that divine ideas and thoughts are concrete universals or we can pull apart abstract and non-intentional and argue that they're abstract intentional objects. Since I think being a universal is sufficient for being abstract, I opt for the second option: divine ideas and thoughts are abstract objects.[34]

Putting the World Together

Due to space limitations, I'll briefly summarize the end result of tasks T2 and T3. As a personal being worthy of worship, God acts for reasons. We might ask then, why did God create? A venerable answer is that God creates to *manifest* his goodness by creating a world that is *full*, *ordered*, and *directed*. Any universe God might create will be *full* of good things, either as full as it could be, or as full as it could be to realize every fundamental *kind* of good thing, or as full as it could be to realize every fundamental *kind* of good thing above some goodness threshold. Since God's goodness is communicated through finite substances in so far as they are *like* God in some way and since a plurality of finite substances of varying degrees of goodness, power, and rationality ordered in the best possible way (with respect to their own end and relative to other beings) more closely reflects God's infinite perfection than a single kind of finite substance (ordered only with respect to its own end), it follows that any universe God might create will include a multiplicity of substances of varying degrees of goodness, power, and rationality ordered in the best possible way along a scale of being. Finally, the good things perfect goodness creates are created *for* God. God is the ultimate *final cause*. This gives us reason to expect any universe God might create will display his manifold goodness along a great chain of beings that is ordered—even finely tuned—for, among other things, the *existence* and

---

34. The Fregean is *partially* vindicated for there *are* some representational abstract objects even if they are not mind-independent.

flourishing of free persons who can freely enter into union with God as their highest good and final end. The above considerations suggest, as an answer to task T2, that God creates according to some version of the *plenitude* and *gradation principles* such that the universe is ordered into a great chain of being directed toward its end in Christ (thus, the scale of being is not a scale of more and less *being*, but rather a scale of greater and lesser *perfections*).

Finally, regarding T3, I suggest that participation can be understood as a three-place relation between God, divine ideas, and finite substances. More formally, taking "shares in the being of" as primitive:

> $P(x,y,z)$ = x shares in the being of y along dimension z, where x is a finite substance, y is God and z is a divine idea.

Strictly speaking, individual substances participate in God (and vice-versa). Loosely speaking, we can also say that the universe, understood as the aggregate of all finite substances, participates in God too. While distinct from God, created substances are tightly bound to God, existing like God yet in a different way, resembling God in some way or another, and "porous" enough to be the locus of divine presence.[35] Thusly understood, the participation relation plays a number of roles in a Christian Platonic metaphysic: grounding created substance's existence, identity, and value, mediating divine presence in the universe, and tightly tying together the created and sacred orders.

Finally, being is univocal. I define "to be" and "to exist" as the *having of a property*.[36] There is a growing body of literature in contemporary metaphysics concerning *ontological pluralism* that helps us see how it is possible to endorse a doctrine of *analogia entis* consistent with the univocity of being and a participatory ontology.[37] If things exist in various ways, as the ontological pluralist claims, then the relevant distinction isn't between *existence* and *being*, but between existing in *this* way or *that* way. Recall that participatory ontologies unite God and created substances into a sacramental whole. On the current proposal, God and created substances both exist in the same sense, but not in the same *way*. God exists as an ultimately fundamental particular whereas created substances exist as dependent fundamental particulars (i.e., they are fundamental with respect to the created order only).

---

35. God and substances are mutually co-inhering in that they are *internally present* to each other even as they are not *intrinsically related* to each other (as parts or aspects or modes).

36. Moreland, *Universals*, 134–39.

37. See for example Kris McDaniel, "Ways of Being," McDaniel, "A Return to the Analogy of Being," McDaniel, "Being and Almost Nothingness," and Spencer, "Ways of Being."

Thus, everything that exists fall within the domain of the unrestricted existential quantifier, ∃x, whereas God and created substances can be said to exist in distinctive modes or ways, and thus fall under distinct restricted quantifiers, say, ∃x_G and ∃x_C.[38] These restricted quantifiers are semantically primitive and more fundamental than the unrestricted quantifier, highlighting the neo-Aristotelian claim that questions of fundamentality are more interesting and revealing than questions of existence in metaphysics. With the notion of *ways of being* in hand, the defender of participatory ontologies can affirm that God and creatures exist in the same sense, even as they exist in distinct modes or ways, and thus can only be spoken about analogically, now understood, as falling under distinct fundamental restricted quantifiers.[39]

Peter and Paul Go to Heaven

Regarding humans, I affirm what C. Stephen Evans and Brandon Rickabaugh dub "significant minimal dualism."[40] As a conscious agent, I am identical to my immaterial soul. My soul is that which grounds personal identity and survives the death of my physical body. My body is a distinct non-separable part of me. As a substance, however, it is also appropriate to say that I am a deep unity of body and soul, even a body-soul composite. I am a bodily soul. The substance that I am picks out what *kind* of being I am, categorically speaking.[41]

I affirm the traditional view of the afterlife. Peter and Paul are bodily souls, particularized natures (i.e., individual substances along with their properties, parts, and powers) that belong to the same substantial kind as determined by their real definition. Upon death, Peter and Paul continue to exist in heaven without being modified in a bodily way.[42] They will reunite with material bodies at the resurrection. The matter that constitutes their

---

38. Here I follow the suggestion of Jeff Brower and his application of the insights from the literature regarding ontological pluralism to Aquinas. See Brower *Aquinas's Ontology of the Material World*, 51.

39. Brower *Aquinas's Ontology of the Material World*, 51.

40. Evans and Rickabaugh, "What Does It Mean to Be a Bodily Soul?"

41. My view affirms, unlike Cartesian dualism, that human beings are a single substance and unlike Thomistic dualism, that I am identical to my soul and not the body-soul composite. I agree, however, with Aquinas that disembodied existence is not the natural state for humans.

42. As Brandon Rickabaugh describes in personal correspondence, upon death, Peter and Paul are still bodily souls but not embodied souls. Also see Rickabaugh, "Dismantling Bodily Resurrection Objections to Mind-Body Dualism."

resurrected bodies need not be continuous with the matter that constituted their pre-resurrection earthly bodies. This is because bodies, as non-separable parts of substances, find their identity in virtue of the (substantial) whole in which they are a part. The human body, like the physical universe, is never wholly physical. A human body without a soul is a corpse. Likewise, a universe without God is a lifeless simulacrum of a universe. The universe in which we live and move and have our being is a sacramental universe, a participatory theatre of God's goodness and glory.[43]

1.2 ARISTOTELIANISM RESPONSE—TIMOTHY L. JACOBS

Introduction

Paul Gould's modified theistic activism (*MTA*) admirably defends historic orthodox doctrines and metaphysical and epistemological realism. I appreciate that he employs a little Aristotle and Aquinas to help *CCP*. He inspires the Christian philosopher by defining his role as one who "seeks an account of the nature and structure of reality that is faithful to Scripture." There is "considerable freedom . . . to bring the truths of Scripture into coherence with the deliverance of empirical evidence," but wisdom will seek the metaphysic that most accurately corresponds to reality (p. 5).

Top-Down Method

Platonism rightly defends realism, but it does so in a top-down approach that says universals are self-subsisting abstract objects, and individuals are secondary participants. Aristotelians work in reverse, similar to good biblical hermeneutics, using what is more clear to understand what is not. Substances (individual beings) are primary and the most real, while universals are abstractions and secondary substances. Aristotelian empiricism can defend the faith as rational by following the evidence wherever it leads. "Faith is the substance [*hypostasis*] of things hoped for, the proof [*elenchos*] of what is not seen" (Heb 11:1). Platonism, on the other hand, favors a coherentist leap of faith and divine command theory. Gould may not hold this,

---

43. Thanks to J. P. Moreland, Brandon Rickabaugh, Richard Brian Davis, Scott Smith, and Ross Inman for helpful comments. This essay was made possible through the support of the Henry Center for Theological Understanding, funded by a grant from the John Templeton Foundation. The opinions expressed in this essay are those of the author and do not necessarily reflect the views of the John Templeton Foundation.

but history shows the dangers. Influenced by Platonism, Cartesian dualism started top-down from the mind and was unable to prove the material world adequately. Later, Berkeley, Hume, and Kant pioneer idealism (named after Plato's forms), phenomenology, and other views that deny the existence or knowability of reality—which continues today. This influences theological presuppositionalism, which holds that reason without grace cannot know reality accurately, and so faith is a leap. Why leap to Christianity instead of another religion? The answer should be reason and evidence. This difference in method leads to the most significant disagreement between Platonism and Aristotelianism.

Abstract Substances

Aristotelianism disagrees that Platonic ideal forms are properties that exist as abstract substances in Plato's heaven. How can a property exist without being a property of something? Properties are not substances. That collapses categories. Forms are proposed to explain how perfection can be known from imperfect sensibles. Aquinas says, "[Plato] is taking on something harder in order to explain something easier, which is unfitting."[44] Other forms would have to be postulated for relations and accidents leading to the problematic "third man" forms to explain Plato's infamous halfway point between sensibles and forms. Aquinas says a simpler option should be preferred if it sufficiently accounts for the existence, knowability, and perfection of things.

Universals become known as observation abstracts similarities between sensibles and subtracts differences, but universals are not themselves substances. Aristotle says we refer to what is *of a subject* (essence), *in a subject* (accidents), or *neither* (the subject itself).[45] The rational nature *of a human* is essential, while the color *in a human* is accidental, and the individual person is the subject. Plato's heaven is unnecessary, nor is it corroborated by Scripture or experience. It is unclear how abstract substances are supposed to relate to each other. Does the universal *living thing* include the universals *plant, animal,* and *human*? Certainly substances can contain parts, but parts are in or of subjects, and are not subjects themselves. Can the universal *human* have the human essence without being a human? Aristotelianism says the essence is not a human because it is the similarity between humans *abstracted from* substances; essences are not themselves substances. Where

---

44. Aquinas, *Commentary on Metaphysics* I.14.
45. Aristotle, *Categories* 1a20.

Plato says the object of knowledge is the universal, Aristotle says it is the external object known by means of universals.

Aristotle says Plato leaves it "an open question" as to how particulars participate in universals.[46] Aquinas adds that Platonists "have not investigated how a common species is participated in by sensible individuals."[47] On the contrary, an individual participates in a universal if it shares a similarity with others. Apples and cherries are a similar color, but redness does not exist apart from them. Your health and my health are different forms shaping different matter, but they share a similarity known as "health." Individuals are primary and universals are secondary, which is why Aristotle calls them primary substances and secondary substances.

Mind-Body Dualism

Gould says, "I am identical to my immaterial soul," (p. 15), and the body is a second substance. I am part of something bigger. Yet, Gould says in an almost Aristotelian formula, "My body is a distinct non-separable part of me. As a substance, however, it is also appropriate to say that I am a deep unity of body and soul, even a body-soul composite. I am a bodily soul" (p. 15). Gould seems to want to have its cake and eat it too. Aquinas agrees that we are a body-soul unity, but that is because a person is a single substance composed of two parts. If two substances combine, they become one substance, as hydrogen and oxygen become water, or they remain separate while connected by accidental relation, like a hand in a puppet. God created us to be essentially physical things. Our body-soul unity is not an accidental relation of two substances. When Jesus became man, he was not a puppeteer as in the Apollinarian heresy. His body is essential, which is why he bodily resurrected and ascended. If "I am identical to my immaterial soul," nothing prevents me from the heresy of reincarnating in a new body, instead of resurrection.[48] Gould is nowhere near these heresies because he affirms orthodox body-soul unity. However, if you have a unity, you have a single substance. Platonism tends to think of the body mechanistically and the soul as its motor. Aquinas replies that this means bodily actions cannot be attributed to the whole person.[49] We cannot say that Peter runs, but that his body runs while his soul does not. The action of a part can only be attributed to the whole if it is part of the essence.

46. Aristotle, *Metaphysics* (987b11–14).
47. Aquinas, *Commentary on Metaphysics* I, lect. 10.
48. Aquinas, Aquinas, *Summa Theologica* II-II.83.11, obj. 5; III.50.4.
49. Aquinas, Aquinas, *Summa Theologica* I.76.1.

All said, Plato is my hero, and his allegory of the cave was my first reading in philosophy. His heroic quest for truth inspired my own. However, in saying abstractions are more real than sensible substances, he made way for others to say that reality must conform to our mind, instead of the other way round. Christian Platonists temper this with doctrine, and in most contemporary battles, they are friends with Aristotelians.

1.3 IDEALISM RESPONSE—JAMES S. SPIEGEL

Paul Gould's chapter on Christian Platonism is instructive and innovative. I am essentially in agreement with Gould's methodological approach to Christian metaphysics, and I heartily affirm his orthodox theological commitments to divine aseity and sovereignty, that God is creator and sustainer of the cosmos while also ontologically distinct from his creation. I also agree that everything in the universe points toward the reality of God. As for Gould's distinctively Platonist commitments, there are aspects of his account which I am happy to affirm, while others I view as problematic. Here I will primarily focus on those aspects with which I disagree.

Gould describes his view as a modification of the "theistic activism" of Thomas Morris and Christopher Menzel, according to which "all abstract objects, including properties and relations [are] constituents in the divine mind" (p. 4). According to Gould, abstract objects exist in two forms. Some of these "exist as uncreated constituents of the divine substance," while others "are not part of or essential to God [but] exist in a distinct realm—call it Plato's heaven, call it the abstract realm, or whatever. The created properties and relations reside in this realm" (p. 4). I see nothing inherently problematic with Gould's view from a *theological* standpoint. That is, there is no apparent tension between the doctrine of divinely created abstract ideas and any core Christian teachings, whether the doctrine of God or any other primary Christian theological commitments. However, Gould's view and approach does present a significant epistemological problem, as I will explain.

The distinctive feature of Gould's *modified* theistic activism is the notion of independently existing abstract objects. Why suppose some abstract objects exist outside of God? What explanatory purpose do these serve that divine ideas cannot? It is important to remember that one of the criteria for assessing metaphysical theories (or any other kind of theory that aims to account for a variety of data) is the principle of parsimony, which Gould himself honors when he cites simplicity or elegance as a truth-indicative theoretical virtue. This is the principle that one should not multiply entities without good and sufficient reason. Clearly, independently existing abstract objects are supposed to explain the occurrence of various instantiations of properties (e.g., red, round, crunchy, sweet, etc.) we encounter in the world. But aren't divine ideas of universals sufficient to account for these things? If so, then positing a realm of abstract ideas outside of God is explanatorily redundant.

Presumably, Gould would say that the separate realm of abstract objects, or "Plato's heaven," really is necessary from an explanatory standpoint. But he offers little in the way of supporting this supposition. While he urges that his brand of Platonism is a "rationally superior metaphysic for the Christian because it is consistent with the deliverances of Scripture . . . and it has . . . the most important theoretical virtues (explanatory scope and power, empirical adequacy)" (p. 5), he never specifies *how* his view demonstrates these virtues. The closest Gould comes to providing an explicit argument for his view is when he appeals to Reinhardt Grossmann's "axiom of localization"

> such that "no entity whatsoever can exist at different places at once or at interrupted time intervals." Rejecting the axiom of localization leads to absurd consequences. For example, in juggling two red balls, the immanent realist is committed to the bizarre claim that the universal *redness*, instantiated in two numerically distinct balls, is both moving away and toward itself when juggled. It is better to hold that abstract objects (i.e., properties) are nonspatially "in" concrete objects as metaphysical parts or constituents. (p. 11)

Gould's appeal to Grossman's axiom of localization, however, is problematic, specifically because it trades on an equivocation of the term "entity." To say that a property is shared by two or more particulars is not to imply that any single "entity" is located in two different places at once. Rather, it is simply to recognize that a particular property (e.g. color, shape, flavor, etc.) has multiple instantiations. And, anyway—given his view—appealing to an abstract realm of universals in this case only adds another dimension where, say, "redness" is located. After all, there is still "redness" in the juggled balls, even granting that there is a perfect, eternal, universal redness in the Platonic realm of abstract objects. Finally, even if some such argument could succeed in showing that abstract objects must exist independently of all of their instantiations in particular objects in the world, a further argument is needed to demonstrate that universals in the mind of God are somehow insufficient to ground or explain the reality of the various instantiations.

Throughout the latter part of Gould's chapter he elaborates his theory by explaining the "three logical moments" of divine activity, specifically *possibilia*, *abstracta*, and *concreta*. While these speculations are interesting and admittedly plausible, these are not compelling grounds for thinking the theory is *true*. We might even go so far as to grant that the first and third categories of divine activity he distinguishes here are intuitively compelling, since concrete physical reality is empirically obvious and the realm of the possible is implied by the fact that humans are divine image bearers. (After all, we constantly dream up possibilities, so presumably God would as well, since he is infinitely more imaginative than we are.) But the reality of a Platonic realm of abstract ideas is hardly so intuitively obvious. Gould has no justification for simply asserting their existence. He must provide evidence or an argument for this crucial claim.

1.4 POSTMODERNISM RESPONSE—SAM WELBAUM

Introduction

Paul Gould's chapter on Christian Platonism is fascinating. His initial description of various forms of Platonism I found helpful, and his methodology is rigorous. One point that delighted me a good deal was that, in the midst of his rigorous thought, there was a clear desire for the universe to be a dynamic, active place, infused with the life, love, and grace of the creator. I resonate deeply with the concept of a "sacramental universe" and loved not just its inclusion, but the label used to describe it as well. Beyond that though, there are three areas of, if not disagreement, confusion. In all three cases, I either don't believe I can sign on with Gould's assertion, don't see the need for the assertion, or don't think that the assertion is clear enough to hold; or perhaps some combination of the three. These three areas are the universe's participation in the divine, the relationship between the body and soul, and the Biggest and the Bigger Bang.

The Universe, Participation, and the Divine

Throughout Gould's chapter there is a tension, an admirable tension, to try and not fall into the classic tropes of Platonism. Part of the genius of Plato's thought was finding a way in which both Heraclitus and Parmenides were right, the former in this world, the latter in the real world. This approach has led to Platonism focusing heavily on the changelessness, or the detachedness of reality. Christianity is a dynamic religion, so shying away from this tendency is helpful. However, on occasion the use of participation terminology begins to sound almost Parmenidean, or even pantheistic/panentheistic. Obviously, this is not Gould's intent, and he even shifts his verbiage at the end of his chapter when he parallels the relation between the soul and the body, with God and the universe. Done the wrong way, this would point to panentheism all the more, but Gould is careful not to make God the soul of the universe, at least not the in the same way that the soul is the soul of the body.

That said, what exactly does Gould mean when he speaks about the universe, or individual substances, participating in God? Gould understands this participation to be the primary relation that joins God to finite substances, and the way in which God gifts being to existent things. "Strictly speaking, individual substances participate in God (and vice-versa). Loosely speaking, we can also say that the universe, understood as the aggregate of all finite substances, participates in God too" (p. 14). I think I can think of three possible ways in which I might understand what Gould is doing here. First, he may just be using the term "participation" in multiple ways. If a substance is gifted being by its participation in God, I don't know what God participating in the existent object means. I wonder if here he means that the object draws being from God, but that God is active in the universe? If this is the case, then the issue is merely one of terminology.

Second, it seems that he might mean this in a manner somewhat similar to the Eastern Orthodox understanding of the divine energies. Perhaps it is not God in his being that is participating in the universe, but rather that God, acts through the power of his energies, which in this case would give being, and those energies are that which the universe participates in, and the means by which God participates in particular substances? Third, it might be that by all substances participating in the divine, and God in all things, Gould is using Platonic verbiage to make sense of Paul's word in Colossians 1, all things are created by him, for him, through him, and held in existence by him. If this is the case, I think my concern is merely with the baggage related to Plato's use of the term "participation" as it would then apply to this chapter, since it seems that Paul and Plato are, as is often the case, saying different things.

In sum, while the idea that substances participate in something greater is standard for Platonism, I wonder here how we can speak of God participating in substances without equivocating on the term. It also seems odd that all substances would participate in God, yet the realm of ideas in Gould's system is located in "Plato's heaven" as opposed to the traditional Augustinian approach in placing them in the mind of God.

Body and Soul

I affirm with Gould that the soul is the ground of personal identity, that it survives death, and while absent from the body exists in a state for which it was not created. I suppose my question though is, "What am I?" On Gould's account my soul grounds my identity, my body is a non-separable part of me, and as a substance I am a body-soul composite. Earlier, when discussing substances, Gould states, "As a fundamental unity, the substance is the ground, its parts, property instances, and powers the grounded." A few sentence later, "Substances *are* particularized natures and they *have* properties" (p. 10). Initially I presumed that Gould was going to say that my soul was my essence, and that when joined with a body it became substance, however, that is not what occurred. I'm left wondering here, am I my soul, and I happen to have a body? My soul who cannot be separated from my body? Or am I my nature, who has as properties a soul and a body? Or perhaps I'm merely my substance, which grounds my nature, which has as parts of it a soul and a body? In any case, once the soul, which grounds identity, stops being "me" and instead is a property, or a part of "me," it becomes hard to understand what I actually am.

It seems as though Gould is attempting to get as close to hylomorphic dualism as a Platonist can, even stating that his understanding of substance is hylomorphic, yet I'm unsure that he does so in a clear way.

The Biggest and the Bigger Bang

Space is brief, so I will present this last section quickly, but when discussing the logical order of creation, Gould posits that in the first logical moment of creation, God creates all possibilities, and in the second, the abstract ideas needed to create physical universe. It is an interesting concept, and it has caused me to ask a series of questions I never thought I would ask. In eternity past, prior to the creation of the universe, did God in his omniscience know the concepts of Nebraska, CEO, BOGO pizza slices, silver medal, piano, etc.? It sounds from Gould's presentation that God did not know these concepts, as they were non-existent and therefore there was nothing to know. (Gould says God "dreams them up" at this moment). Once created they were known fully. If this is the case, first, it's a bold move for a Platonist to hold to something that might constitute a change in the divine (based on Hellenistic understandings of change), but second, is there a reason for the opposite to not be the case? Is there a reason not to presume that God created based on the ideas that have been eternally in his mind? Further, is there a reason for him to create a realm of ideas exterior to himself, particularly if created beings are participating in him? Couldn't the ideas be in him, and have always been in him, without need of creation? Here my first and third questions have connected and I hope in his rejoinder Gould is able to provide more clarity.

1.5 PLATONISM REPLY—PAUL M. GOULD

Introduction

My dissertation was on God's relationship to abstract objects. More recently, I've been very interested in exploring metaphysical accounts of concrete material reality. The invitation to contribute to this book offered me an opportunity to combine the abstract and concrete realms of reality into a unified whole, under the banner of Christian Platonism. It's the kind of thing I'd be more comfortable doing in another decade or so. Metaphysics is hard! Still, one must follow the opportunities where they lead, so I happily jumped on board with this project, eager to defend realism regarding abstract objects, given its relative unpopularity of late.

This project has been invigorating. My fellow contributors have pressed me to articulate and defend my view. I've learned a lot from reading about their take on reality too, even when I disagree. The philosophical back-and-forth encapsulated in this book represents part of what is best and the most fun about philosophy and being a philosopher: defending your mature views amongst friends. (It is only part of what is best and most fun: becoming wise, or becoming like Christ, as we pursue knowledge and wisdom for the flourishing of all is the heart of Christian philosophy.) While we differ on the details, we are united around the core convictions of historic Christianity. Our common convictions are greater than our differences. This is an in-house debate between Christian philosophers. As stated in my lead essay, I don't think there are many knock-down arguments that show one view as obviously false in metaphysics. Still, we can argue for the rational superiority of our view and so I turn, in this final essay, to respond to objections raised to my version of Christian Platonism.

Can Divine Ideas Do Everything Platonic Properties Can Do?

James Spiegel asks, "Why suppose some abstract objects exist outside of God? What explanatory purpose do these serve that divine ideas cannot?"

(p. 19). Since, according to Spiegel, divine ideas can explain everything that Platonic abstract objects can, the latter are "explanatorily redundant" (p. 20).

Let's take stock. Both Spiegel and I agree that properties exist, (at least) some of them are universals, and that they are abstract objects. Our difference lies in the characterization of these objects in our mature theories. I opt to give them (relative) fundamental existence and locate them in a distinct-from-God abstract realm. Spiegel is content to identify these objects with divine ideas. Since Spiegel thinks his view is explanatorily on par with mine yet more parsimonious, we have no good reason to posit a distinct-from-God Platonic realm of abstracta. I deny that theistic idealism is explanatorily equivalent to Christian Platonism. Perhaps surprisingly, I also deny that it is more parsimonious than Christian Platonism. Before I make my case, I first set aside a red herring.

Spiegel notes that "the closest Gould comes to providing an explicit argument for his view [that properties are Platonic] is when he appeals to Reinhardt Grossmann's 'axiom of localization'" (p. 20). He then goes on to argue that my appeal to the axiom of localization is problematic since it "trades on an equivocation of the term 'entity'" (p. 20). He continues, "To say that a property is shared by two or more particulars is not to imply that any single 'entity' is located in two different places at once. Rather, it is simply to recognize that a particular property (e.g., color, shape, flavor, etc.) has multiple instantiations" (p. 20). In reply, recall that I appeal to the axiom of localization in my discussion of the difference between Platonic or transcendental realism and Aristotelian or immanent realism. According to the immanent realist, the universal redness is multiply located at two different locations in space at the same time when it is instanced in the red truck and the red ball. For the immanent realist, contrary to Spiegel's claim, the very same entity *is* located at two different places. There is no equivocation on the term "entity." This is the price of admission for the immanent realist: the same entity is multiply located at different places. I think this too steep a price to pay. Better to hold, as I do, that the universal redness is non-spatially "in" concrete objects.

But none of this really matters when it comes to the dialectic between the theistic idealist and the Christian Platonist. The issue is not about *how* concrete particulars have their properties, but whether or not properties are identified with divine ideas.

Now consider the issue of explanatory scope and power. Do divine ideas explain the characteredness of charactered objects? I doubt it. As I have noted in my reply to Spiegel's lead essay, ideas *mediate* between mind and world, they do not play the structure-making role. Properties are intentionally inert. Concepts, of course, are not. It is a category mistake to employ divine ideas as world-builders. Divine ideas aren't constituents of concrete particulars and they don't explain the characteredness of charactered objects (see also my worries about bundle-theoretic accounts of concrete particulars in my initial reply to Spiegel in section 3.2 below). Christian Platonism is superior to theistic idealism in explanatory power and scope.

Suppose I am wrong and that divine ideas explain the character of charactered objects as well as Platonic properties do. Does theistic idealism win, in virtue of being the more parsimonious theory? No. There are at least two kinds of parsimony to consider. There is *ontological* and *ideological* parsimony. Even if we grant that theistic idealism is more ontologically parsimonious, in virtue of having one less *kind* of thing on its ontological list, it is not more ideologically parsimonious. For now, ideas are not essentially intentional and properties are not essentially structure-making. Why then, do divine ideas play the role of structure making? They just do. Consider finite particulars (let's set aside the unloveliness of assaying the divine being on this account). On the one hand, if the idealist says divine ideas just do play the structure-making role, he appeals to brute facts, and the theory becomes ideologically less parsimonious than Christian Platonism (since, on my view, I can appeal to the nature of properties to explain why they structure the world). On the other hand, if the idealist says that divine ideas structure-make because God wants it that way, we must ask, why does God want it that way? Either God has no reason, in which case, it is just a brute fact that divine ideas structure-make, or God has a reason. If God has a reason why he wants it this way, I think it would be something like the following: "because God prefers ontological parsimony to ideological parsimony" (for we are left with an unlovely and less ideologically parsimonious disjunctive account of the nature of divine ideas as either structure-making or mind-world mediating). But it is not obvious to me that God prefers ontological parsimony to ideological parsimony. It seems equally plausible, given what theologian Andrew Davison describes as "the riotous diversity of creation,"[50] that God prefers ontological generosity over ontological parsimony or that God prefers the optimal balance of ontological and ideological parsimony and that balance is obtained by (as I think) creating three fundamental beings to ground all distinct-from-God reality.

Summing up. I don't think theistic idealism is explanatorily superior to Christian Platonism. Moreover, even if it were, I don't think it is more parsimonious, all things considered. But even if it were, I'm not sure that would count against Christian Platonism. God has created a beautiful, complex,

---

50. Davison, *Participation in God*, 33.

awe-inspiring, wonder-filled universe. This should lead us to resist the contemporary impulse toward desert landscapes in metaphysics.

Top-Downism

Jacobs claims that Platonism employs a "top-down approach that says universals are self-subsisting abstract objects and individuals are secondary participants" whereas "Aristotelians work in reverse, similar to good biblical hermeneutics, using what is more clear to understand what is not" (p. 16). Jacobs is doubly mistaken. First, recall from my lead essay my description of top-downism as "the idea that the explanatory principles for any metaphysical theory about reality are derived from the spiritual or intelligible or divine realm" (p. 8). In his book *Aristotle and Other Platonist*, Lloyd Gerson makes a persuasive case that Aristotle and Plato were in substantial agreement with respect to top-downism.[51] In other words, Aristotle is a Platonist. According to Gerson, the main elements of Platonism that were thought to be in harmony with Aristotle's writings include the ideas that the universe has a systematic unity, this systematic unity is hierarchical, and that the divine and intelligible realm is a fundamental, irreducible, and necessary explanatory category for the universe.[52] Thus, it is false that Plato employs a top-down approach whereas Aristotelianism employs a bottom-up approach. Both were instances of top-downism and, as Gerson notes, the only true opponent to them was the "bottom-upism" of the materialist or atomist (and in our day, the microphysicalist or the neo-Humean).[53]

Second, recall the taxonomy of Platonisms from my lead essay. I made it clear that I was not defending traditional Platonism, but rather a more fine-grained version of Platonism called contemporary Christian Platonism. Whatever traditional Platonism thought about "subsisting abstract objects" and "secondary participants," I have no use for such language. On my version of Christian Platonism, substances are fundamental wholes and property instances are non-separable parts of these fundamental wholes (and properties are metaphysical parts of properties instances). Moreover, my neo-Aristotelian account of substances as well as my defense of Platonic properties is largely driven by a kind of empiricist (and particularist) epistemology such that the "more clear" help us to understand what is less clear. There is no

---

51. Gerson, *Aristotle and Other Platonists*.
52. Gerson, *Aristotle and Other Platonists*, 32–34.
53. Gerson, *Aristotle and Other Platonists*, 32.

reason to claim that Aristotelianism, but not Platonism, "can defend the faith as rational by following the evidence wherever it leads" (p. 16).[54]

The caricature gets worse, unfortunately, for Jacobs writes that Platonism "favors a coherentist leap of faith and divine command theory" (p. 16) that has historically led to all kinds of dangerous errors including Cartesian dualism, idealism, phenomenology, relativism, theological presuppositionalism, and fideism. Whereas Welbaum's lead essay lays all the ills of society at the feet of modern philosophy, Jacobs seems to locate them in Plato's commitment to top-downism! I'm not sure where to begin. I don't think traditional Platonism endorses a "coherentist leap of faith" and it certainly doesn't endorse a divine command theory. Even if it did, these would not be core tenets of Platonism but auxiliary hypotheses that Platonists are free to accept or reject. The problem is not Platonism or top-downism. The problem is bottom-upism, along with its resultant materialism, reductionism, and scientism. Platonism and Aristotelianism are in agreement against this foe (or to state this in another way, the Christian Aristotelian should endorse something like *AD* and *SU*).

Abstract Substances?

Jacobs finds it inconceivable that properties could exist without being "*in a subject*." Since I claim that properties can exist apart from their exemplification, it follows, according to Jacobs, that I'm treating them as a kind of substance. "How can a property exist without being a property of something? Properties are not substances. That collapses categories" (p. 17). I agree that properties are not substances. But I disagree that to say they can exist without being a property of something is to "collapse categories." While I adopt a substance-attribute framework, as I explained in my lead essay, I don't think that substances are the only (relative to this world) fundamental kind of entity. Aristotle thought that "if primary substances did not exist it would be impossible for any of the other things to exist (*Categories* 2b5)."[55] Fair enough. I've shown how it is not impossible. Merely asserting the authority of Aristotle does not show my view as impossible, nor does it provide a reason to think I've collapsed any categories. This charge misses its mark by failing to address my distinctive position and claims.

---

54. As I briefly state in my lead essay, my argument for Platonic realism begins by noting two *empirical* facts—qualitative and resemblance facts—and then reasons to belief in abstract objects as the best explanation for these facts. For more see Gould "There Are Universals," 247–259.

55. *The Complete Works of Aristotle*, 5.

The same can be said for the contemporary Christian Platonist's motivation for belief in abstract objects. This time citing Aquinas, we are told that "Forms are proposed to explain how perfection can be known from imperfect sensibles" (p. 17). While that may have been a motivating factor for Plato, it is not (or need not be) for the contemporary Platonist. For me, the chief *philosophical* reason for positing Platonic properties is that they offer the best solution to the problem of universals. Platonic properties are the best explanation in terms of ontological and ideological economy for the observed qualitative and resemblance facts in the universe. It is not enough to simply report Aristotle's position and then declare "Plato's heaven is unnecessary, nor is it corroborated by Scripture or experience" (p. 17). Jacobs has demonstrated none of this. I've offered reasons for my view and I believe that it is consistent with both Scripture and experience. Moreover, Jacobs has not clarified his account of the metaphysics of properties. It is notoriously difficult to determine whether Aquinas was a nominalist or realist about properties. I think that Jeff Brower is closest to the truth in thinking that Aquinas was a (moderate) realist with respect to the medieval problem of universals given his commitment to individual common natures but a nominalist with respect to the contemporary problem of universals given his denial of abstract objects.[56] What does Jacobs think is the best way to go here? No arguments have been offered for why nominalism is superior to realism or, what account, if any, he thinks is needed to endorse belief in common natures. (Brower thinks Aquinas endorses two types of sameness, numerical and internal, and opts for common natures that are numerically distinct yet internally the same.) It is not enough to assert a line from Aristotle or Aquinas as evidence for their all-things-considered position, let alone as the rationally preferred position over competitors.

Bodily Souls

Jacobs notes that, when it comes to human persons, I "seem to want to have [my] cake and eat it too" (p. 18). Yes, Yes! Please! Jacobs thinks I'm endorsing a two-substance view of human persons, but I'm not. I'm offering a hylomorphic account of human persons. A human person is a soul that has (as a non-separable part) a physical body. Again, much of Jacobs' reply is spent arguing with something close to the standard take on traditional Platonism, but it misses the target when it comes to my view and the Christian Platonism I defend. To wit, "Platonism tends to think of the body mechanistically and the soul as its motor" (p. 18). Perhaps. By that is not my

---

56. See Brower, "Aquinas on the Problem of Universals," 715–35.

view! I am a bodily soul, a deep unity of soul and body, a functional whole. When in the disembodied state, I'll still be a bodily soul (as I stated in my lead essay, I'll be a disembodied bodily soul) waiting for the resurrection of the body and the new heaven and the new earth. But it will be me—not a part of me, as the Christian Aristotelian view suggests—that waits.

Welbaum perceptively asks if, on my account, I am a soul or nature. This is a good question because, as Welbaum rightly points out, there are places within my lead essay that seem to suggest both. My reply: *qua* person or agent, I am a soul that has a body. *Qua* substance, I am a particularized nature, a single substance with a real definition. Strictly speaking "I" am identical to my soul. That is *who* I am. When it comes to *what* I am, I am a particularized nature, a rational animal, a hylomorphic substance. Hylomorphism is the doctrine that substances are compounds of matter and form. My account of substances counts as an instance of hylomorphism. I define a *substantial form* or *nature* as a metaphysical principle that is the objective cause of something's being the entity that it is and *substantial matter* as any non-separable part, property instance, or power of a substance whose existence and identity is defined by the substance as a whole.[57] Following Aristotle, I do not understand the form-matter compound mereologically such that a substance is one thing composed of two parts. Rather, I've provided a non-mereological gloss of substances such that the substantial form is not a part of a substance but rather the unifying principle of a substance (hence, my language that substances just *are* particularized natures). When it comes to human persons, the body-soul relationship is also to be understood in these terms: the soul is the substantial form of an organic, living, body.[58] I am a soul, a bodily soul.

Participation

Welbaum wonders what I mean, exactly, when speaking about the universe, or individual substances, participating in God. He suggests three possible interpretations, none of which I endorse (although I think Paul's language in Colossians is consistent with my participatory account). In my lead essay, I give an account of the participation relation as a three-place relation between God, divine ideas, and finite substances. The participation relation is a *relation*, joining together two distinct things. But it is an *asymmetrical*

---

57. For more on my neo-Aristotelian account of substances, see my "Neo-Aristotelian Accounts of Divine Creation."

58. For a helpful discussion of hylomorphism along these lines, see Marmodoro and Mayr, *Metaphysics: An Introduction to Contemporary Debates & Their History*, 33–39.

relation. God shares, creatures receive. In his work on the metaphysics of participation, Andrew Davison describes the asymmetry of the participation relation as follows:

> the core idea of participation is that things are what they are by participation in God: they are what they are because they receive it from God. Whenever participation is invoked, however, the parallel idea in the doctrine of God usually lies close at hand: that if having by participation is the mark of the creature, then having (or being) without derivation is the mark of God.[59]

Thus, I'm not using, at least in this essay, "the term 'participation' in multiple ways" (p. 22), as Welbaum suggests. Rather, I'm acknowledging the *asymmetry* of the participation relation at the heart of a Christian Platonic metaphysic: God and creature participate in each other but in different ways. God is participated-in, creatures participate-in.

The Logical Moments of Divine Creative Activity

Finally, Welbaum wonders if prior to creating the universe, God knew "the concepts of Nebraska, CEO, BOGO pizza slices, silver medal, piano, etc." (p. 23)? I answer in the affirmative and hope in my very brief reply to clear up some confusion. I distinguish three *logical* moments in God's creative activity. In the Biggest Bang, God freely and spontaneously dreams up all general and singular concepts (including the concepts in Welbaum's list) and all possible worlds (understood as conjunctions of propositions). If God is timeless, then the concepts and propositions God dreams up are part of God's temporally unextended life. If God is temporal, then the concepts and propositions God dreams up are everlastingly dreamed up in a single instance. If God did not have the concept of Nebraska, then, given divine omniscience, there would be no concept of Nebraska. There is no conceptual landscape "beyond" the one dreamed up by God in the Biggest Bang. As Leftow puts it, "what God conceives determines what is conceivable."[60] Thus, God has his concepts and propositions "from eternity" past, before the creation of the physical universe at the Big Bang. Welbaum asks, "Couldn't the ideas be in him, and have always been in him, without need of creation?" (p. 24). This idea has a venerable history, to be sure. Unfortunately, I don't think that you can get the full panoply of concepts and propositions from the divine nature alone, hence the need to dream up

---

59. Davison, *Participation in God*, 22.
60. Leftow, *God and Necessity*, 290.

possible individuals and worlds. (How are we supposed to get the concept of Nebraska or BOGO pizza slices from the divine nature? While so-called deity theory might be sufficient for some general *types* and *general* concepts, it isn't sufficient to generate possible *individuals* and *singular* concepts.) Finally, the reason why God creates a distinct-from-God realm of abstract objects—not abstract *ideas* as Welbaum mistakenly writes—is because, as noted above in my reply to Spiegel, divine ideas/concepts mediate between mind and universe whereas Platonic properties (and relations) play a role in structuring the universe.

BIBLIOGRAPHY

Anderson, James N., and Greg Welty. "The Lord of Noncontradiction: An Argument for God from Logic." *Philosophia Christi* 13.2 (2011) 321–38.

Aquinas, Thomas. *Commentary on the Metaphysics*. Translated by John P. Rowan. 1961. Reprint, Chicago: Dumb Ox Books, 1995.

———. *Summa Theologiae*. Translated by Brian J. Shanley, O.P. Indianapolis, IN: Hackett, 2006.

Aristotle. "Categories." In *The Complete Works of Aristotle*, Vol. I, edited by Jonathan Barnes. Princeton, NJ: Princeton University Press, 1984.

———. "Metaphysics." In *The Complete Works of Aristotle*, Vol. I, edited by Jonathan Barnes. Princeton, NJ: Princeton University Press, 1984.

Boersma, Hans. *Heavenly Participation: The Weaving of the Sacramental Tapestry*. Grand Rapids: Eerdmans, 2011.

Brower, Jeff. "Aquinas on the Problem of Universals." *Philosophy and Phenomenological Research* 92.3 (2016) 715–35.

———. *Aquinas's Ontology of the Material World*. Oxford: Oxford University Press, 2014.

Crane, Tim. "Intentionality as the Mark of the Mental." In *Contemporary Issues in the Philosophy of Mind*, edited by Anthony O'Hear, 229–51. Cambridge: Cambridge University Press, 1998.

Davis, Richard Brian. *Beyond the Control of God? Six Views on the Problem of God and Abstract Objects*. London: Bloomsbury, 2014.

Davison, Andrew. *Participation in God*. Cambridge: Cambridge University Press, 2019.

Evans, Stephen C., and Brandon L. Rickabaugh. "What Does It Mean to Be a Bodily Soul?" *Philosophia Christi* 17.2 (2015) 315–30.

Gerson, Lloyd P. *Aristotle and Other Platonists*. Ithaca NY: Cornell University Press, 2005.

Gould, Paul M. "Neo-Aristotelian Accounts of Divine Creation." In *Divine Causation: Essays in Philosophical Theology*, edited by Gregory E. Ganssle. London: Routledge, forthcoming.

———. "Properties and Universals." In *Philosophy: A Christian Introduction*, James K. Dew, and Paul M. Gould, 104–15. Grand Rapids: Baker Academic, 2019.

———. "Theistic Activism and the Doctrine of Creation." *Philosophia Christi* 16.2 (2014) 283–296.

———. "There are Universals." In *Problems in Epistemology and Metaphysics*, edited by Steven B. Cowan, 247–59. London: Bloomsbury Academic, 2020.

Gould, Paul M., and Richard Brian Davis. "Modified Theistic Activism." In *Beyond the Control of God? Six Views on the Problem of God and Abstract Objects*, edited by Paul M. Gould, 51–64, 75–79. London: Bloomsbury, 2014.

———. "Where the Bootstrapping Really Lies: A Neo-Aristotelian Reply to Panchuk." *International Philosophical Quarterly* 57.4, (2017) 415–28.

Grossmann, Reinhardt. *The Existence of the World: An Introduction to Ontology*. London: Routledge, 1992.

Jubien, Michael. "Propositions and the Objects of Thought." *Philosophical Studies* 104 (2001) 53–54

Keller, Lorraine Juliano. "The Argument from Intentionality (or Aboutness)." In *Two Dozen (or so) Arguments for God: The Plantinga Project*, edited by Jerry L. Walls and Trent Dougherty, 11–28. Oxford: Oxford University Press, 2018.

Leftow, Brian. *God and Necessity*. Oxford: Oxford University Press, 2012.

Marmodoro, Anna, and Erasmus Mayr. *Metaphysics: An Introduction to Contemporary Debates and Their History*. Oxford: Oxford University Press, 2019.

McDaniel, Kris. "Being and Almost Nothingness." *Nous* 44.4 (2010) 628–49.

———. "A Return to the Analogy of Being." *Philosophy and Phenomenological Research* 81.3 (2010) 688–717.

———. "Ways of Being." In *Metametaphysics*, edited by David Chalmers, David Manley, and Ryan Wasserman, 290–319. Oxford: Oxford University Press, 2009.

Menzel, Christopher. "Theism, Platonism, and the Metaphysics of Mathematics." In *Christian Theism and the Problems of Philosophy*, edited by Michael D. Beaty, 208–29. Notre Dame, IN: University of Notre Dame Press, 1990.

Moreland, J. P. "Exemplification and Constituent Realism: A Clarification and Modest Defense." *Axiomathes* 23.2 (2013) 247–59.

———. *Universals*. Montreal: McGill-Queen's University Press, 2001.

Morris, Thomas, and Christopher Menzel. "Absolute Creation." *American Philosophical Quarterly* 23 (1986) 352–62.

Morris, Thomas V. *Anselmian Explorations: Essays in Philosophical Theology*. Notre Dame, IN: University of Notre Dame Press, 1987.

Plantinga, Alvin. "Augustinian Christian Philosophy." *The Monist* 75.3 (1992) 291–320.

———. *Where the Conflict Really Lies*. Oxford: Oxford University Press, 2011.

Plato. "Sophist." In *Plato: Complete Works*, edited by. John M. Cooper. Indianapolis: Hackett, 1997.

Rickabaugh, Brandon. "Dismantling Bodily Resurrection Objections to Mind-Body Dualism." In *Christian Physicalism? Philosophical Theological Criticisms*, edited by R. Keith Loftin and Joshua R. Farris, 295–317. New York: Lexington Books, 2018.

Rodriquez-Pereyra, Gonzalo. "Nominalism in Metaphysics." *Stanford Encyclopedia of Philosophy* (2015), edited by Edward N. Zalta. https://plato.stanford.edu/entries/nominalism-metaphysics/.

Schaffer, Jonathan. "On What Grounds What." In *Metametaphysics: New Essays on the Foundations of Ontology*, edited by. David J. Chalmers, David Manley and Ryan Wasserman, 366–73. Oxford: Oxford University Press, 2009.

Schindler, David C. "What's the Difference? On the Metaphysics of Participation in a Christian Context." *The Saint Anselm Journal* 3.1 (2005) 1–27.

Smith, James K. A. "Will the Real Plato Please Stand Up?" In *Radical Orthodoxy and the Reformed Tradition: Creation, Covenant, and Participation*, edited by James K. A. Smith and James Olthuis, 61–72. Grand Rapids: Baker, 2005.

Spencer, Joshua "Ways of Being." *Philosophy Compass* 7.12 (2012) 910–18.

Temple, William. *Nature, Man and God: Being the Gifford Lectures Delivered in the University of Glasgow in the Academical Years 1932–1933 and 1933–1934*. London: Macmillan, 1934.

Taylor, Charles. *A Secular Age*. Cambridge: Harvard University Press, 2007.

van Inwagen, Peter. "God and Other Uncreated Things." *Metaphysics and God: Essays in Honor of Eleonore Stump*, edited by Kevin Timpe, 3–20. London: Routledge, 2009.

Wolterstorff, Nicholas. *On Universals*. Chicago: University of Chicago Press, 1970.

Yandell, Keith. "God and Propositions." In *Beyond the Control of God? Six Views on the Problem of God and Abstract Objects*, edited by Paul M. Gould, 21–35, 46–50. London: Bloomsbury, 2014.

2

Christian Metaphysics and Aristotelianism

- 2.1 Aristotelianism—Timothy L. Jacobs
- 2.2 Platonism Response—Paul M. Gould
- 2.3 Idealism Response—James S. Spiegel
- 2.4 Postmodernism Response—Sam Welbaum
- 2.5 Aristotelianism Reply—Timothy L. Jacobs

2.1 ARISTOTELIANISM—TIMOTHY L. JACOBS

Introduction

Where does knowledge begin? Mom points to "car," "train," "tree," "rock." Young Peter points to a double-trailer semi-truck, "train?" "No." He catches similarities from many experiences then forms toys with playdough. Square and triangle are similar because they are both shapes. Red is the same kind of thing as black but different from tree. Each of these answers "What is it?" by referring to similarities and differences while presupposing the real first object of knowledge, that a thing or a being is present. Metaphysics is the study of *being itself,* or *being as being*.[1] This chapter introduces Aristotelian metaphysics from a Christian perspective with help from Thomas Aquinas.

---

1. Special thanks to my wife Marian Jacobs for her feedback. She is a wonderful writer herself. Thanks also goes to my proofreaders Andrew Cuff, Dustin Bryant, Joshua Harris, Steven Jensen, Elliot Polsky. I always try to surround myself with my betters. Any remaining flaws are my own.

Being as Substance

"My oatmeal is too hot," Peter says. Mom puts an ice cube in it. Peter understands something is hot or cold, and he refers to this *substance* separately from its temperature. He has a *subject* he describes with a *predicate*. The oatmeal is hot, thick, etc. The oats' incidental qualities change without changing the essential substance or identity—oats. These qualities are called *accidental forms* and the change *accidental change*.[2] A form answers "What is it?" by describing qualities. Aquinas calls forms a thing's "whatness" (*quidditas*) after Aristotle's "what it was to be [a certain thing]."[3] In order to say a subject changes, it must persist through change, being present before, during, and after. The oats are hot then cold. Its qualities change, but its identity remains the same.

"Where do oats come from?"

"Dirt."

"What happens after I eat them?"

"They turn into you."

While oats take different forms, such as a plant or cereal, at some point we call that form something else, like dirt or a person. The oats are gone, but by the conservation of mass,[4] the matter is still there. When dirt becomes oats then a boy, we say the substance, or identity, changed in *substantial change* because its *substantial form* changed.[5] The substantial form is the form of qualities essential (not accidental) to the identity of the individual thing. When oats becomes a boy, the identity "oats" is gone, replaced by "boy." It is the boy who plays in the sandbox, not oats. Peter in his sandbox knows half a pile of sand is still sand, but half his dog is not a dog. The oats, the dog, and the boy are more than just the sum of their parts. They have their own distinct identities as substances. But if a subject persists through change, what subject persists through substantial change? When we say *it* changes identity from being oats to a boy, what is *it*?

When oats becomes a boy, the underlying carbon, water, etc., persists through change. Carbon and water have a separate identity when they are a lump of coal or a glass of water. When carbon is subsumed in a larger

---

2. Aristotle, *Physics* 192b9–193b20; Feser, *Scholastic Metaphysics*, 164.

3. "Quidditas," Aquinas, *Summa Theologica* I.84.7. Aristotle, *Metaphysics* 1029b, τὸ τί ἦν εἶναι. All four causes, Aristotle, *Metaphysics* 983a; 988a.

4. The law of conservation of mass in physics states that mass is neither created or destroyed. With Einstein's theory of special relativity, we know that mass and energy are convertible, but conservation remains. *What* changes from mass to energy? What is conserved? Prime matter.

5. Aristotle, *Categories* 2a11–18.

substance, it is no longer simply a lump of carbon. Since the boy is not simply carbon and water, he is more than the sum of his parts. Carbon is no longer the main subject as an independent thing. It is *virtually present* within the boy, subsumed into a larger subject with his own unique identity, actions, and abilities.[6] Predicates are now said not of carbon but of the boy. Carbon may still revert to being its own subject if it separates from the boy. By contrast, a chair is just wood with no new essential powers. The power of sight is said of the boy in a way that it cannot be predicated of oats or carbon. A severed hand or corpse no longer act in their characteristic ways, so they are no longer human. We say they *were* human but are now only decaying piles of carbon.[7] Materialism sees no difference between substantial or accidental form. Since carbon in the boy is no longer a separate individual thing, it is not the subject that persists before, during, and after substantial change. In accidental change, oats are hot then cold. Substantial change is not carbon changing from oats to the boy or else the boy would be an accidental form, and we could say carbon plays in the sandbox just as we say oats is hot or cold. Substantial change is not a change of quality but of identity. If no subject persists through substantial change, we have not change but annihilation and creation.

The subject of substantial change cannot be the smallest particle. We think of identity apart from what it identifies, shape apart from what it shapes, or form apart from what it *en*forms.[8] The smallest particle cannot be merely form or merely matter, but if matter changes form, then we must be able to talk about matter abstractly without form, even though whenever matter exists, it has a substantial form. Just as the form *coin* shapes copper, copper in turn shapes matter, and we can abstractly think of "copper" and "matter" separately while knowing real matter (not abstracted) must be copper or nickel or photon or some other substantial thing composed of matter and form. We need a new term to refer to matter apart from form that persists through substantial change, so we call it *prime matter*.[9] It does

---

6. Aquinas *Summa Theologica* I.76.4, ad 4. For a detailed discussion on understanding the proper identity and form of elements in relation to the human body see Decaen, "Elemental Virtual Presence in St. Thomas" and Clarke, *The One and Many*, 72–74; Feser, *Aristotle's Revenge*, 307–74.

7. Aristotle, *De Anima* 412b17–22.

8. "*Enform*, From Latin *informare*, Anglo-Norman *enfourmer*. III.a To give form or determinant character to; b. to give a thing its essential quality or character; to animate; c. Of a soul, life, etc.: to impart life or spirit to; to animate. "inform, v" (*Oxford English Dictionary Online*). More precisely, forms cannot be understood apart from reference to their proper subject, e.g., "shape" implies "of an object," unless one is Platonic and views forms as self-subsistent. See also Aquinas, *Expositio super Boethium De Trinitate* 5.3.

9. "Something must have existed as a primary substratum from which it should come and which should persist in it," Aristotle, *Physics* 192a31.

not exist as a thing or a substance any more than matter exists without form. It is what persists through changing from being *this* to *that*. Since change requires a subject to persist before, during, and after change as the subject we say changed, prime matter persists through substantial change. Otherwise, matter would be annihilated and created, which violates physics. Since this first subject persists through substantial change, it has the *potential* to be any kind of substance.

Aristotle called the ever-present union of form and matter *hylomorphism*.[10] By contrast, Plato thought form could exist separately from matter in the realm the of forms. Since a substance is an individual thing as a subject, we can talk about *kinds* of substances, like Peter and his dog. "Human" is not an individual thing but a similarity between Peter and his mom. Aristotle called the individual thing a *primary substance* and its kind, *secondary substance*, also called essence, (human) nature, or species.[11] In short, a primary substance is a thing, and a secondary substance is a universal.[12]

What Are Universals?

When Peter notices he and his mom are similar but different from his dog, he observes "human" by subtracting their differences. Likewise, the similarity between red and brown is color, and square and triangle are shapes. The difference between a form and a universal is that a universal is a similarity between forms. Peter's health is an accidental form of him, not his mother. He does not possess her health, but "health" is a concept applying to both of them, even if the cause of health may be different diets. Likewise, the triangularity shaping a traffic cone does not make a pizza slice triangular, but we talk about their similarity in geometry without talking about traffic cones and pizza slices. Adding a slice of pizza adds another form, but not another universal. Five slices have five forms and one universal. In hylomorphism, an individual thing is composed of form and matter, not a universal similarity and matter. Since universals refer to kinds of forms, *universal* and *form* are sometimes confused. If Peter's identity persists after death, then his form must remain distinct from his mother's even while their humanity is not.

10. ὕλη, matter; μορφή, form; Aristotle, *Metaphysics* 987b. Aquinas, *Summa Theologica* I.84.7.

11. Aristotle, *Categories* 2a11–14, 2a5; Aristotle, *Physics* 192b33–34. For an in-depth explanation of substance, see Wippel, *The Metaphysical Thought of Thomas Aquinas*, chapters 7–9.

12. For a detailed look at how Aristotelian-Thomistic physics and metaphysics is compatible with and corrective of modern physics, see Feser, *Aristotle's Revenge*; Wallace, *The Modeling of Nature*; Barr, *Modern Physics and Ancient Faith*.

Similarities, or universals, become more inclusive as we subtract more differences. Lassie and Odie are dogs. Dogs and horses are animals. Plants, animals, and humans are living things. We eventually reach Aristotle's set of irreducible universals, called categories: *substance, quality, quantity, when, where, relation, affected, affecting (action), position, possession.*[13] The exact number and definition is not pressing, though the distinction between substance and the rest (nine accidents) distinguishes between a subject and predicates, between substantial form and accidental form.

The categories are *limited* because one does not contain the same universals as another. "Brown" is not in the same category as "standing" or "noon." If we subtract any more differences, we will be left with descriptions that are *unlimited* because they apply to all substances, or beings. *Being* thus becomes the most inclusive universal. Four aspects of being that apply to all things are the *transcendentals—being, one, true,* and *good*—which Plato and Aristotle referenced but were developed systematically by Augustine, Boethius, Avicenna, Aquinas, etc.[14] They are *convertible* because they are different names of the same subject teasing out various ways of understanding being, as a man may be father and husband. Anything is a thing (being, substance) with a whatness (*quiddity*, form) and unity (one) that can be understood (true), and has perfect order or leads to it (good). A dog's color (category) says nothing of its size (category). But when we say what kind of being it is, we know something true about it, it has unity, and this description is some kind of order. This implies all being is good, evil is privation or lack of being and not a substance, the universe is intelligible, and God's essence is simple without parts and convertible with his existence. Since all categories and transcendentals describe *being*, then *being itself, being unqualified,* or *being as being,* is the subject of metaphysics.[15]

ABSTRACTION AND THE PROBLEM OF UNIVERSALS

When "brown" or "triangle" is understood, logicians refer to *understanding* universals, or simple apprehension, as the first act of the mind. When we combine universal terms we form propositions with the second

---

13. Aristotle, *Categories* 1b25–2a4.

14. Aristotle, *Metaphysics*, books I and X; *Nicomachean Ethics*, book I; Aquinas, *Quaestiones Disputatae de Veritate* 1.1, 21.1–3. Beauty is sometimes included as a transcendental, but most properly it is the same as Good; Aquinas *Summa Theologica*, I-II.27.1, ad 3.

15. Aristotle, *Metaphysics* 1002a22, 982a5, 1026a31, 1333a17–33.

act—*judgment*.[16] *Reason* is the third act, moving from proposition to proposition in an "argument."

If universals refer to properties in objects, in what sense are they real? This is called the problem of universals.[17] There are three general answers.[18] First, *Platonic realism* claims universals are independent objects in the realm of the forms, or intelligible realm.[19] Since a pizza slice and a traffic cone are not perfect triangles, then the perfect form of triangle is in another realm. Triangularity would exist even if all triangular things ceased since it exists as its own immaterial object. Since we understand perfection but do not see it in the world, knowledge begins with the mind, not external reality, and learning is remembering what we knew when we lived in the realm of the forms before birth. Aristotle's view critiques Platonism. Where Plato treats forms as real objects, Aristotle treats them as predicates or descriptions of subjects.[20]

Second, *nominalism*, as taught by William of Ockham, claims universals are conventional names grouping individual things and are not real. "Dog" as a universal refers to all individual dogs. A universal is a set, group, or amalgamation. If universals only refer to individuals, then how do we group Lassie and Odie under "dog" but leave out a horse? Without the ability to distinguish similarities, then it is unclear how groups are formed. Nominalism cannot group things together without sneaking in dependence on real similarities.[21]

Third, Aristotle's *hylomorphism*, sometimes called moderate realism, is a mean between Platonic realism and nominalism. As stated above, universals refer to real similarities in things with differences subtracted, but not as separately existing immaterial forms. Physical things are forms enforming matter, so their similarities do not exist separate from them. The act of extracting similarities and leaving behind differences is known as *abstraction*.[22] It is an action unique to reason, a power of the human soul to be discussed after defining metaphysics as a science.

---

16. Aristotle, *Metaphysics* 1011b25; *Quaestiones Disputatae de Veritate* 1.1.

17. This is also usually equated with the problem of the one and the many. See Clarke, *The One and Many*, 92–108. See also Wippel, "Participation and the Problem of the One and the Many."

18. Jensen, *The Human Person*, 138.

19. Plato, *Republic* 504d–511e; 514a–518d.

20. Although I hint at critiquing Platonism (as well as nominalism, materialism, and many other issues) throughout this chapter, I defer more specific critiques to my responses following the other chapters in this book as these issues arise.

21. Jensen, *The Human Person*, 139.

22. Aquinas, *Summa Theologica* I.84.1, I.85.1–4.

Metaphysics and The Order of the Sciences

A science consists of a subject, principles (premises), and conclusions.[23] The subject of metaphysics is *being itself*, or *being as being*.[24] Principles may be axioms common to all sciences, like noncontradiction and causality, or proper to a particular science, like definitions and suppositions. Conclusions become the subject of the next higher science. The order of the sciences is an extension of the learning process.

In contrast to Plato, Aristotle says we are born a blank slate (*tabula rasa*)[25] without knowledge. This still allows for natural habits and disordered intellect or passions, which Aristotle acknowledged is present at birth, and Aquinas attributed to original sin.[26] Some ideas are present potentially in our power of reason, waiting for experience to awaken them, such as self-evident axioms of logic or the first precept of natural law (i.e. "do good and avoid evil"). Learning begins through sensory observation of the physical world.[27] Effects are observed before causes are demonstrated. The order of discovery in epistemology is usually the reverse of being in metaphysics. Confusing this leads to problems in every area of philosophy.[28] Crime inves-

---

23. Aristotle, *Parts of Animals* 72a.; Houser, "Essence and Existence in Ibn Sīná," 213. Note that Ibn Sīná is also known as "Avicenna." For more detail on the science of metaphysics and the order of the sciences, see Wippel, *The Metaphysical Thought of Thomas Aquinas*.

24. Aristotle, *Metaphysics* 1002a22, 982a5, 1026a31, 1333a17–33.

25. Aristotle, *De Anima* 430a1, "γραμματείῳ ᾧ μηθὲν ἐνυπάρχει"; Aquinas, *Commentary on Aristotle's De Anima* III.4, "*tabula, in qua nihil est actu scriptum.*" Being born without knowledge does not mean being born without nature or inclination. Biblically, we are born with an inherited disposition to sin, variously called original sin or depravity (Romans 5:12, 19). This refers not to a knowledge we have from birth but to a disordered will lacking in virtue.

26. Aquinas says we are born with some natural habits (Aquinas, *Summa Theologica* I-II.51.1) but are born having virtue potentially and not actually (Aquinas, *Summa Theologica* I-II.63.1; Aristotle, *Nicomachean Ethics* 1103a14–1103b1). "Sin nature" from original sin is a kind of second nature or habit and cannot corrupt man's essential nature (Aquinas, *Summa Theologica*, I-II.82.1; 85.1, 6). Otherwise he would undergo substantial change.

27. His definition of truth is conformity of intellect to thing (Aristotle, *Metaphysics* 1011b25; Aquinas, *Quaestiones Disputatae de Veritate* 1.1).

28. For example, Descartes starts from the mind and is unable to prove that the external world is clearly and distinctly real. "I do not find, from the distinct idea of corporeal nature that I find in my imagination, that any argument can be supposed, that I can necessarily conclude the existence of any body," René Descartes, *Meditations* 6.3, (my translation of, "nondum tamen video ex eâ naturae corporeae ideâ distinctâ, quam in imaginatione meâ invenio, ullum sumi posse argumentum, quod necessariò concludat aliquòd corpus existere"). Descartes goes on to claim mathematics is clear

tigators collect evidence and work backward to discover a cause, but causation works the other way. This is how scientists discovered the principles of gravity, electromagnetism, and weak and strong nuclear force. Likewise, Aristotle discovered four fundamental principles, known as the four causes: material, formal, efficient (agent), and final (end, purpose, order).[29] They respectively ask "What is it made of?"[30] "What is it?" "What is the source of change or stability?" and "What is its end or completion of change?"[31] We have already discussed matter and form. Taking after Pythagoras, Plato thought these two explained the source and end of change, but Aristotle recovered agent and end from the Presocratics.

Since knowledge starts with observation, Aristotle orders three basic sciences by degree of reference to matter: physics, math, and metaphysics.[32] What we call *metaphysics* he calls *philosophy* or *theology*. Almost everything discussed in this chapter Aristotle calls physics or one of its sub-sciences. His work on logic in the *Organon*[33] become principles in *Physics*, which develop anthropology in *On the Soul*, then *Nicomachean Ethics*, which is completed in *Politics*. Metaphysics studies being, principles (e.g., noncontradiction and causality), intellect and truth, substance and essences, and God.

Aquinas says metaphysics, or philosophy, rests on principles learned from human reason. He separates theology as the next and last science. Aquinas' defense of theology as a science pioneered modern systematic theology. Just as metaphysics depends on, continues, and partially includes physics, theology also accepts, includes, and develops philosophy. In addition to principles and conclusions inherited from philosophy, theology includes biblical revelation among its premises. Its subject is God, and its

---

and distinct. Aristotle, by contrast, says we know of physical bodies first then mathematics later because it refers to physical bodies. Cartesianism influenced the idealism of Berkeley, Hume, Kant, etc. This "modern problem" as it is often known is nicely dealt with by Wittgenstein as explained by Kenny in *Wittgenstein*.

29. Aristotle, *Physics* 194b24–195a3; Aristotle, *Metaphysics* 983a24–b5. For a modern defense and explanation of the four causes, see the chapter titled "Causation," in Feser *Scholastic Metaphysics*, 88–159.

30. Matter secondarily asks "What persists through change?" Properly, this secondary question leads to the primary question.

31. The Presocratics asked about what changes, what the source of change is, and what persists through change, or form, agent, and matter respectively. Thales thought water to be the prime substance that persists. Heraclitus thought fire, Anaximenes air, Xenophanes water and earth, and so on. Plato and Aristotle note the consensus as matter. Aristotle, *Metaphysics* 987a.

32. Aristotle, *Physics* 184a17; Aristotle, *Metaphysics* 1026a19.

33. The *Organon* is the collection of *Categories, On Interpretation, Prior Analytics, Posterior Analytics, Topics, Sophistical Refutations*. For the introductions to Aristotelian logic, see Kreeft *Socratic Logic* and Houser's *Logic as a Liberal Art*.

conclusions are doctrine.[34] Theology includes and builds on philosophy to finish what philosophy starts without undermining it.[35]

The Physics of Souls

We can categorize kinds of substances with the help of five predicables Porphyry explains in his *Introduction* to Aristotle's *Categories*: genus, species, difference, property (proper accident), and accident.[36] Since a substance is an individual subject, the predicables describe its qualities or forms. A *species* (secondary substance, definition, or nature) is a *genus* plus a *difference*. As universals are similarities with differences subtracted, species is a universal essence with individuation subtracted. For example, Human nature (species) is the rational (difference) animal (genus).[37] A genus is a universal with the "difference" subtracted, and is like a more inclusive universal or category.

The distinction between the substantial and accidental forms of an individual are not to be confused with the further separation of accidental forms into properties and accidents. *Properties* arise from the essence (species) and are always present. Since the definition of a triangle, as Euclid says, is *three-sided plane figure*, it has the property of its angles always summing to 180 degrees. Since humans are rational, they are morally responsible and know good and evil.[38] *Accidents* are qualities that may or may not be present, as in hair color. One may define an essence indirectly through its properties or accidents. Humans may be called *political* (property) *animals* (genus) or a pet dog a *canis* (genus) *familiaris* (domesticated, accident). The

---

34. Aquinas, *Summa Theologica* I.1.2; I.1.4.

35. Theology's dependence on philosophy mirrors faith's rationality, or else we have no reason to believe and faith is irrational. We have reason to believe the Bible (philosophy), then use it as reason to believe doctrines (theology). Since this scheme says truth is correspondence to reality, it conflicts with coherentist presuppositional epistemology and divine command theory.

36. Porphyry, *Introduction*.

37. Many do not like calling humans a kind of animal due to associations with evolution. However, "rational animal" refers only to the fact that humans have animal-like bodies but still have distinctly human immaterial minds and souls, as will be shown. Even if a human does not actually reason due to infancy or illness, they are still the same kind of thing, the same species. Since reason is the distinguishing trait for humans, the perfect use of it is a life of wisdom. Aristotle calls this final cause "the end, that for the sake of which a thing is done," or as Alasdair MacIntyre differentiates, "man-as-he-is" and "man-as-he-could-be-if-he-realized-his-telos." *After Virtue*, 54. See also Aristotle, *Physics* 195; Aristotle, *Metaphysics* 1013.

38. Genesis 2:9.

Bible defines humanity as the image of God by explaining its role to fulfill the "cultural mandate," which depends on human reason.[39] Because man is rational, he has a will, which is fulfilled in loving God.[40] All else in human nature is physical and not shared with God, including passions, which are attributed to God anthropomorphically.[41]

Using the five predicables, we can reconstruct Porphyry's Tree to categorize substances. Since universals are similarities with differences subtracted, the Tree works in reverse, starting from the most universal and adding differences to define species. Modern scientific classification uses this system more extensively. First, being is divided into substance and accident. Substances are divided into material and immaterial (i.e., spirits). Material can be animate (living things) or inanimate (elements). Animate things are defined by having the power of life, the vegetative power, acting in growth, nutrition, and reproduction.[42] Some living things have the difference *sensation*, the five senses, and these are animals. Sensation yields pleasure and pain and thus the appetitive power (emotion) and sometimes locomotion. Of things with animal bodies, some have the power of reason, which are humans.

Since humans are composed of form and matter, their powers (abilities, faculties) are qualities of their substantial forms. As we learn of effects before causes, we also see actions and then identify powers. Humans have all five powers of living things: vegetation, sensation, appetite, locomotion, and reason[43]—describing one overarching substantial form defined by its most distinctive power, reason. Any substantial form that includes the vegetative power is called the *animating principle* of that thing—in Latin *anima*, in Greek *psyche* (ψυχή), and in English *soul*. Since plants and animals have the vegetative power, they also have "souls" in a broad sense. Yet, since they

---

39. Genesis 1:26–30, cited in Aquinas, *Summa Theologica* I.93.1. Aquinas says being in God's likeness must relate not to genus but to difference, which is rationality (Aquinas, *Summa Theologica* I.93.2). The image of God is not merely intellect or else angels would have it more than man, but the image of God also includes certain properties unique to man (Aquinas, *Summa Theologica* I.93.3). Image may refer to essence, degree of conformity to grace, or perfected knowledge and love of God. All humans have the first, Christians the second, and postmortem perfected Christians the third (Aquinas, *Summa Theologica* I.93.4).

40. The will as an intellectual power will be mentioned again later. Ecclesiastes 12:13 says the end of humanity is to keep God's commands. In John 14:15 Jesus says, "If you love me, keep my commandments." See note below on the chief end of humanity being knowledge of God. Philippians 3:10.

41. Genesis 1:26–28; 2:9; 3:5. See Psalm 18 for physical and personality anthromorphisms.

42. Aristotle, *De Anima* 412a14; 415a25.

43. Aristotle, *De Anima* 414a30; Aquinas, *Summa Theologica* I.78.1

are different kinds of substances—different forms of life—they have different kinds of "souls": vegetative soul or sensitive (sentient) soul.[44]

Because matter and form have the relationship of potentiality and actuality, the substantial form defines what subject actually exists. Since the soul is the substantial form, Aristotle calls it the first actuality of the kind of physical body that can support life.[45] The matter enformed by the soul cannot be simply a pile of carbon and water. It must be organized with the mechanisms needed to sustain life—those of an organism. God formed man out of dust, then breathed life into him.[46] He is more than a pile of dirt, more than the sum of his parts.

In hylomorphism, a person is a whole composed of substantial form (soul) and matter (body). The Aristotelian soul is not to be confused with the dualist ghost possessing a body like a motor that is a substance existing distinct from the body. Substance dualism in Plato or Descartes struggles to connect mind and body because they are seen as separate substances. This "mind-body problem" is helped if we point to the whole person, the unity that includes these two substances. But this would mean the whole is a substance, and soul and body become elements of it, bringing us back to Aristotelian hylomorphism. Since substantial form cannot exist separately from matter, Aristotle's psychology cannot see how souls persist after death. However, Aquinas develops Aristotle's claim that intellect is immaterial and impassible to demonstrate the immortality of the soul.[47]

Aristotelian Psychology

Besides the vegetative power, things with animal bodies have sensation, both external (sight, hearing, smell, touch, taste) and internal (common sense, imagination, estimation, memory).[48] Unlike Plato, for whom knowledge begins in the mind, Aristotle and Aquinas are sense realists, who believe knowledge begins with external senses. The terminology of internal "sense" can mislead because we usually use "sense" to mean external senses. The

---

44. It is interesting that the Old Testament uses *nephesh* (נֶפֶשׁ) to refer to all sentient things, animals and humans both, but not plants (Genesis 1:20; 2:7). It may also be why the New Testament, written in a Greco-Roman context quite influenced by Plato and Aristotle, often mentions soul along with spirit or mind for clarification (Matthew 22:37; Hebrews 4:12).

45. Aristotle, *De Anima* 412a27, 14

46. Genesis 2:7.

47 Aristotle, *De Anima* 414a20, 408a27, 429b5.

48. Aristotle, *De Anima* 424b20 ff.; Aquinas, *Summa Theologica* I.78.3–4.

internal senses are the physical operations of the nervous system processing information gained through external senses.

After external senses detect color, sound, etc., *imagination* represents them by internal visualization or imaging in a phantasm (image), however vague. Imagination is not creativity—an act of practical reason. *Memory* retains phantasms, recalling them later. The *estimative power* apprehends whether something is dangerous or desirable, like a beaver fleeing a fox.[49] By themselves, external senses give a chaotic kaleidoscope of disconnected sense data. *Common sense* unites them into a common object or experience. Common sense is not wisdom, basic know-how, or street smarts, as in common English.

From sensation arises the sensitive appetite—the power of concupiscible and irascible emotions, including pleasure and pain, desire and fear, love and anger, etc.[50] Although we often consider imagination and emotion as thoughts of our minds, the sensitive and appetitive powers arise within physical bodies, and must be bound to physical organs, like the brain. Dogs, which are purely physical, have dreams and emotions, but they do not *understand* that they do. They cannot think about thinking. Virtue in Aristotelian ethics is the intentional habituation of disordered passions to follow wisdom. Hellenism influenced New Testament language to depict daily ethical struggle as a battle between disordered "passions of the flesh" and wisdom, or between lists of vices and virtues (i.e., the fruit of the Spirit).[51] Emotion interacts with reason in subtle and complex ways in both the foolish and the wise, but it arises from a power distinct from reason.

The intellectual power is divided into cognition (thinking) and will. The three acts of the mind are understanding, judgment, and reason. Since reason includes the others, intellect and reason are sometimes used interchangeably. The will acts in seeking perfection found in happiness[52] in

---

49. Jensen, *The Human Person*, 56.

50. Aristotle, *De Anima* 414b4–15; Aquinas, *Summa Theologica* I.81.2.

51. The fruit of the Spirit contrasted with a list of vices is a classic Greek virtue/vice list formula (Galatians 5:16–25). See also Jacobs, "Virtue/Vice Lists." The Greek singular *karpos* (καρπὸς, fruit) in Galatians 5:22 may refer to various effects of singular grace, or a collective singular, as in, "That tree bears much fruit," instead of "That tree bears many fruits."

52. Flourishing, *eudaimonia* (εὐδαιμονία); blessedness, *makarios* (μακάριος). Aristotle uses *eudaimonia* and *makarios* interchangeably where Jesus uses *makarios* (beatitude, blessedness). For example: εἰ δ' οὕτως, ἄθλιος μὲν οὐδέποτε γένοιτ' ἂν ὁ εὐδαίμων, οὐ μὴν μακάριός γε, ἂν Πριαμικαῖς τύχαις περιπέσῃ. "And this being so, the happy man can never become miserable; though it is true he will not be supremely blessed if he encounters the misfortunes of a Priam" (Aristotle, *Nicomachean Ethics* 1101a5–7). Μακάριοι οἱ πτωχοί, "Blessed are the poor" (Matt 5:3). μακάριος ἀνὴρ οὐ

accordance with virtue[53] fulfilled in knowledge of God.[54] The will uses free-will[55] to choose various means to this ultimate end, where evil is the choice of inordinate means.[56]

Thomistic Epistemology

When sensation takes in the forms of external things, like color, form is received in a nonphysical way insofar as the vision of red does not make the eye red. When red is internally visualized, imagination with common sense forms the phantasm of red and not green. The form of red in the phantasms is the same form of red in external objects, but instead of enforming matter, it is present in a nonphysical way. We can imagine red and green, and we know these refer respectively to the color of a flower or pickle. An imagined triangle and a pizza are similar shapes that a ball is not, so the form in the world is now in the phantasm.[57]

Although phantasms contain nonphysical forms, these forms are restricted by matter in two ways. First, imagination receives forms in all their particularity, not distinguishing similarities from differences, essence from accidents. Triangle is a universal, but an imagined triangle is either acute, right, or obtuse. While we understand the universal as none of these, we always imagine it as one of these. Like material things, phantasms have similarities and differences united. Second, phantasms reside in bodily organs, primarily the brain. Some action besides imagination is needed to abstract similarities from phantasms and leave behind differences. *Abstraction* is the job of the intellect, and that power is called *active intellect*, or *agent intellect*. Just as memory stores phantasms, the intellect also stores

---

οὐ μὴ λογίσηται κύριος ἁμαρτίαν, "Blessed is the man against whom the Lord will not count his sin" (Romans 4:8).

53. See previous notes on Fruit of the Spirit.

54. Paul says a Christian's life purpose is "that I may know him," Philippians 3:10, and this is the perfection (τετελείωμαι, from root *telos*, or end/perfection/final cause) we press on towards and is sought by the mature (τέλειοι, from *telos*). Philippians 3:12, 15.

55. Free-will here need not refer exclusively to libertarian contra-causal free-will but may also refer to compatibilist free will. Interpretation of Aquinas is disputed, though Catholic thought favors libertarianism. See Aquinas, *Summa Theologica* I.83.1, especially ad 3. Emphasis here is on the difference between the necessary willing of happiness arising from synderesis and the choice of means constituting moral choice.

56. Aristotle, *Nicomachean Ethics* 1098a16; Aquinas, *Summa Theologica* I–II.1–3; Galatians 5:22–23; Aristotle, *Metaphysics* 980b22; *Nichomachean Ethics* 177a11–18; *Summa Theologica* I–II.3.8; Philippians 3:10; Genesis 3:5; 1 John 2:15–17.

57. Aquinas, *Summa Theologica* I.84.1; 86.1; Jensen, *The Human Person*, 188.

abstracted universals in the *potential intellect* or *passive intellect*, so called because it potentially knows all universals and passively receives them from the active intellect.[58] When the universal is removed from particularity, it is entirely immaterial in understanding. Dualism and hylomorphism agree that intellect is immaterial.[59] Therefore, the power of reason must be as well, and since the soul is the form containing all powers, it must be immaterial. How did we make this jump? If the soul is the form of the body and contains physical powers too, how can it be immaterial?

Immaterial Rational Soul

In Platonic dualism, the soul and body are different substances, and the person is the soul, not the whole. When Peter sees, his soul sees. To say the body sees is to say something else sees. In materialism, the soul is nothing more than the arrangement of chemicals, implying that it is the carbon that sees. In hylomorphism, the person is a physical body where the whole form is more than the sum of its parts, united by its substantial form, called a soul. It is the person who sees, not the soul or the body alone. This whole can act in many different ways, represented by five basic powers. Humans are different from animals because of reason. As stated above, the intellect can *potentially* know all universals and similarities in physical reality. Whether a finite mind ever *actually* does is another matter.

In order for an eye to see any color, the pupil must be transparent. If it were tinted red, it would see red and not other colors. As Aquinas says, if a fever makes the tongue bitter, everything tastes bitter.[60] The presence of a form prevents the senses from perceiving other forms.[61] The presence of physicality in the intellect would prevent it from potentially understanding universals that refer to all physical things. Since imagination is bound to the physical brain, it is limited. We understand the universal "triangle" but can only imagine a particular triangle. If the intellect were bound to the physical organ of the brain, it would be unable to distinguish the abstracted similarities from the particularities and differences. It would be indistinguishable from imagination.[62]

---

58. Aristotle, *De Anima* 429a10–430a9; Aquinas, *Summa Theologica* I.79.2–3, 86.1; Aquinas, *De Ente et Essentia* 4.1–2.

59. Aquinas, *Summa Theologica* I.77.5.

60. Aquinas, *Summa Theologica* I.85.6; See also Aristotle, *De Anima* 429a18–b5; Aquinas *Quaestiones Disputatae de Anima* 14.

61. Aquinas, *Summa Theologica* I.75.2, 5; Jensen, *The Human Person*, 188.

62. Aquinas, *Summa Theologica* I.75.2, 3; I.77.5; Jensen, *The Human Person*, 185–86.

Neurological data showing brain activity when thoughts occur poses a potential counterargument. Yet, correlation does not imply causation, and such data proves another point. Aquinas knew we use the brain to think, and brain damage impedes reason because it is the organ for imagination and other internal senses.[63] Reason requires the brain in this life because it not only abstracts from phantasms but also uses them when thinking about universals. We cannot help imagine a particular triangle, even while understanding that it is not the same as the universal definition.[64] Immaterial reason makes use of imagination and its organ, the brain, but if it were reduced to the brain, the universal would be indistinguishable from the imagined particular.

Since intellect cannot be limited by being an operation of the brain, it is immaterial.[65] It is simple and not composed of parts like physical bodies. Physical bodies can be destroyed because they are made of parts that can be separated. Intellect is immaterial, simple, and cannot be destroyed (incorruptible). Therefore, it continues to exist postmortem.

Life after Death

How does the immaterial soul accord with hylomorphism's claim that the soul is the substantial form of the body? The soul is the form of all that the body is, from the length of Peter's hair to his power of reason. For brute animals, nothing survives death. The separated human soul loses everything physical, including all powers shared with animals: vegetation, sensation, appetite, and locomotion. This implies the loss of emotion, but not of the will nor the satisfaction that attends it. Without the brain we lose imagination, which would pose a problem for reason only if it depended entirely on it.[66]

Aquinas says that separated souls begin to understand in a way proper to their new mode of existence without a body. Instead of directing universals to particulars, souls will understand them in themselves without reference to particulars.[67] For the faithful, the soul will be filled with knowledge

63. Aquinas, *Summa Theologica* I.84.7.
64. Aquinas, *Summa Theologica* I.84, ad 1; I.85.1, ad 1, ad 2.
65. Aquinas, *Summa Theologica* I.75.6, 76.1.
66. Aquinas, *Summa Theologica* I.89.1.
67. Aquinas, *Summa Theologica* I.89.3, 5. Aquinas says the separated soul knows in a way that is similar to angels without imagined phantasms. Angels, Aquinas thinks, need not be discovered through revelation alone but may be postulated from natural reason. Using Porphyry's Tree, it is easy to see a hierarchy of being ranging from inanimate things through plants, animals, and humans as more powers become present and

of God. Although it once knew incompletely as in a dim glass, it will then know him fully.[68]

Since a human's substantial form is the form of the body, the separated human soul is not a complete substance. It is form without matter. It is still the form of a particular body, but without that body it is incomplete. The soul of Peter is the form of *his* body and not Paul's body, so he cannot reunite to any body but his.[69] Otherwise there would be no problem with reincarnation. However, since the soul is the form of the body, if it enformed a new body, it would undergo substantial change and lose its identity. Besides being unacceptable in orthodoxy, reincarnation is impossible for hylomorphism, but not a problem for Platonic dualism.[70] Hylomorphism sees the soul as permanently related to a particular body and unable to unite to another body.[71]

A human is the kind of thing that has a body, so without a body, a separated soul has an incomplete essence. The disembodied soul of Peter is not the full Peter.[72] Although postmortem the apostle Paul is full of the presence of God, he hopes for resurrection and sees it as essential doctrine.[73] Eternal punishment requires soul and body.[74] Being the form of the body does not mean the soul must enform the exact same molecules. During life, molecules come and go from the body without the person losing their form or identity. Resurrection need not be of the same molecules. Nevertheless, since the soul is the form of a particular body, the Bible implies we will have the same recognizable bodies in the resurrection patterned after Jesus' resurrection body.[75]

---

less dependent on physical bodies. If humans are composites of soul and body with the reason being immaterial, it is not difficult to postulate the existence of immaterial minds with no physical component.

68. Aquinas, *Summa Theologica* I–II.3.8; "For now we see in a mirror dimly, but then face to face. Now I know in part; then I shall know fully, even as I have been fully known" 1 Corinthians 13:12 ESV.

69. Aquinas, *Summa Theologica* I.76.1.

70. See Plato, "Phaedo."

71. *De Ente et Essentia* 2.4.

72. See Aquinas, *Summa Theologica* II–II.83.11, obj. 5; III.50.4.

73. 1 Corinthians 15:12–49.

74. Matthew 10:28.

75. 1 Corinthians 15; Philippians 3:21; 1 John 3:2. The disciples recognize Jesus in his resurrection body (Luke 24:31; John 21:1–12), so long as they were not supernaturally prevented from it (Luke 24:16), and was physical "flesh and bones" which a spirit does not have (Luke 24:39). Aquinas defends the necessity of the resurrection (Aquinas, *Summa Theologica*, Suppl. 27.1), that it must be of the same body or else it is not a resurrection but a new incarnation (79.1), that the particular matter ("ashes") need not

Essence and Existence; Divine Simplicity and Trinity

Although Aristotle holds strictly to hylomorphism, he acknowledges intelligence to be immaterial.[76] According to Aquinas, all beings, including non-hylomorphic immaterial angels, are composed of essence and existence.[77] Essence answers "What is it?" but not "Does it exist?" Aquinas says, one can think of a phoenix without knowing whether it exists.[78] Something other than essence must explain its existence because a phoenix does not exist by definition. The same is true for humans and angels.[79] All essence-existence composites are contingent, depending on another for their existence.[80] This cannot go on forever. Leaning dominos must lean on something steady. It cannot be turtles all the way down. Something must exist by definition, by its essence. For this one thing, essence and existence are the same,[81] convertible, "and this we call God," Aquinas says.[82] This is the historic orthodox doctrine of divine simplicity.[83] Aristotle called this the "first cause" or "unmoved mover" and maintained its simplicity as well.[84]

---

be the same because they are accidental, are not permanent, and "ebb and flow" (79.3, 80.5), otherwise all the matter that passed through his body would resurrect and he would have too much matter.

76. Aristotle, *De Anima* 412b9, 414a20, 408a27, 429b5. See Aristotle, *De Caelo* 310a34. See Bradshaw's chapter "The Prime Mover" in his *Aristotle East and West*.

77. "Every composite has a cause, for things in themselves different cannot unite unless something causes them to unite. But God is uncaused." Aquinas, *Summa Theologica* I.3.7. See also *De Ente et Essentia* 4.7. For an in-depth discussion of the essence-existence distinction and its relation to the problem of universals, see Wippel's chapter, "Essence-*Esse* Composition and the One and the Many," in Wippel, *The Metaphysical Thought of Thomas Aquinas*.

78. *De Ente et Essentia* 4.6.

79. Aquinas, *Summa Theologica* I.50.1; *De Ente et Essentia* 4.10.

80. Saying the existence of all things depends on God (Genesis 1:1; Isaiah 66:2) means he is their cause, not that his existence *just is* their formal existence. God is pure being, but he is not universal being (Aquinas, *De Ente et Essentia* 5.2). This avoids pantheism, as found in Spinoza and many religions.

81. *De Ente et Essentia* 4.6, 4.7, 5.1, 5.2.

82. Aquinas, *Summa Theologica* I.2.3.

83. Aquinas, *Summa Theologica* I.3. Bradshaw, *Aristotle East and West*, 4, 26; Aristotle, "Protrepticus," 270c–d, B63–86. Limited space prevents a biblical theology of divine simplicity, but one can start with monotheism (Deuteronomy 6:4), impassibility (Malachi 3:6), creator (Genesis 1:1; John 1:1–18), existence as essence ("I am," Exodus 3:14), aseity and eternality (Genesis 21:33; Psalms 90:1–2, 102:25–27; Isaiah 40:28–31; Revelation 1:8, 4:11), etc. See also Aquinas' defense of divine simplicity in *Summa Contra Gentiles*.

84. We can partially say what God is without saying that he is, which is why Anselm's ontological argument fails. Whereas Aquinas works from effect to cause, Anselm

With his existence and essence convertible, God is not a composite. His substance must be immaterial, simple, eternal, intelligent, necessary (aseity), and unchanging.[85] Is God composed of Father, Son, and Holy Spirit? The New Testament affirms one God and the deity of all three persons.[86] The Nicene Creed (AD 325, 381) reconciles three with one by affirming divine simplicity—the three persons are one *homoousios* (ὁμοούσιος, essence, being, or substance). Since "person" in Aristotelianism normally refers to the whole substance, Aquinas points out the doctrine of the persons of the Trinity refers to a single substance with three inherent relations.[87] Aquinas' explanation of *homoousios* defends orthodoxy against the heresies of modalism (Sabellianism), monarchianism, psilanthropism, and tritheism. Some may object that God is not simple because he is love, truth, etc. These refer back to God's single substance, just as all the transcendentals refer to one object, being, from different angles.

Aquinas uses hylomorphism to defend the hypostatic (ὑπόστασις, *hypóstasis*) union of Christ. The Chalcedonian Definition (AD 451) says Christ's divine and human natures are distinct, but he is "one person and one subsistence." Anything done by either nature is done by the whole person. Dualism says every human is two substances and the person is the soul, not the body. It is uncertain whether there is unity between these substances and whether the unity can be referred to as an overarching whole person as in hylomorphism where there is one substance, the whole man Jesus. Whatever one part of man does, the whole does.[88] Aquinas explains how the hypostatic union rules out Arianism, Apollinarianism, docetism, Nestorianism, monophysitism (Eutychianism), and others.

---

works from contingent to necessary. We cannot prove God analytically from definition alone, but from his effects. As stated earlier, much confusion arises from forgetting that discovery and causation, epistemology and metaphysics, usually work in opposite directions. For Aquinas' five proofs for God, see Aquinas, *Summa Theologica* I.2.3. See Aquinas, *Summa Theologica* I.2.1 for Aquinas' critique of Anselm's ontological argument. For more on divine necessity and aseity, see *De Ente* 4.6–7, 5.1–2. For an excellent explanation of Aquinas' five proofs addressing modern critique, see Feser, *Five Proofs for the Existence of God*.

85. Aristotle, *Metaphysics* 1075a5–10; See Bradshaw, *Aristotle East and West*, 37. It is beyond the scope of this chapter to defend this list of historic and orthodox divine traits.

86. God is one (Romans 3:30; 1 Corinthians 8:6; James 2:19). All three persons are divine (1 Corinthians 12:4–6; 2 Corinthians 13:13–14; Ephesians 4:4–6; 1 Peter 1:2; Jude 20–21). Trinitarian Baptism (Matthew 28:19). Deity of Christ (John 1:1–4, 20:28; Colossians 1:15–23; 2 Peter 1:1).

87. Aquinas, *Summa Theologica* I.29.4.

88. Aquinas, *Summa Theologica* III.2. Aquinas provides a detailed defense and commentary of the Chalcedonian Definition.

Case Study: Peter and Paul

To summarize the Aristotelian-Thomistic approach to Christian metaphysics, let us take the apostles Peter and Paul as a case study. Since we can answer "What is it?" (essence) without answering "Does it exist?" (existence), Paul's existence is contingent, depending on something other than his essence and ultimately on God as the first cause.

What are Peter and Paul? Through abstraction we observe their similarities and subtract their differences to see that they are human. It is not a nominalist reference to a multiplicity, nor a Platonic subsistent immaterial form. Peter and Paul are subjects, primary substances, whose similarity is the human essence, or secondary substance. Their essence is in them and not separate from them. The apostle Paul is a hylomorphic composite of form enforming matter, united as a single substance. His changing age or health are accidental changes. If a subject changes into another subject, as when dirt becomes oats then a boy, it undergoes substantial change, a kind of change Paul never goes through.

Humans are different from animals because they have reason. Biblically, this is why they are in the image of God. Moral responsibility and the cultural mandate are properties of reason. The form of Paul includes the basic powers of life, and this form is called his "soul." A soul is not a substance separate from the body, as in dualism, because matter is always united to form. Since reason understands universals, which are unlimited by the particularity of matter, then Paul's rational soul is immaterial and incorruptible. When he dies, this part persists, leaving behind physical powers.

Since a human is a physical thing, disembodied Paul has an incomplete essence, but he remains individual because his soul is the form of his body to be resurrected, not another body. Postmortem Paul has the full knowledge of God proper to humans, but he looks forward to the resurrection taking after Christ's, without which our hope is in vain.[89]

2.2 PLATONISM RESPONSE—PAUL M. GOULD

Introduction

My position has much in common with the Aristotelian, especially when it comes to concrete material reality. I'm broadly Aristotelian when it comes to (finite) substances although I give a Platonic gloss of how Aristotelian substances have their (Platonic) properties and I largely agree with Jacobs'

---

89. 1 Corinthians 15:16–19.

hylomorphic account of substance and substantial change. My quibbles lie elsewhere.

Divine Simplicity

According to Jacobs, every substance, or being, that exists is one, true, and good and that "[t]his implies all being is good, evil is privation or lack of being and not a substance, the universe is intelligible, and God's essence is simple without parts and convertible with his existence" (p. 39). As stated, the implication from the unity and goodness of finite substances to the doctrine of divine simplicity is unclear. We are given an argument later, thankfully: "All essence-existence composites are contingent, depending on another for their existence" (p. 53). Since there are contingent substances—"essence-existence composites"—and since you can't have an infinite regress of contingent substances, there must be a necessary substance, a substance without composition, that grounds the causal chain. Thus, "something must exist by definition, by its essence" and "for this one thing, essence and existence are the same" (p. 51). The key premise in this argument, found in a footnote referencing Aquinas, is as follows: "Every composite has a cause, for things in themselves different cannot unite unless something causes them to unite. But God is uncaused" (p. 51, fn. 77, Aquinas, *Summa Theologica*, 1.3.7). In reply, I simply deny the key premise. And why not? It is not the case that every composite has a cause, for God is a composite, yet God exists uncaused. God is, as Jacobs notes, a necessary being. I can stop the regress without appeal to divine simplicity.[90]

I think the real worry regarding composite objects is found in a sentence just before the one Jacobs quotes from the *Summa Theologica*. It runs as follows: "every composite thing comes after its components and depends on them."[91] If part-priority holds such that composite things metaphysically depend on their parts or properties, then if God is a composite thing, God would depend on his parts or properties, violating the doctrine of divine aseity. But God exists *a se*, thus he must not have parts or properties. I endorse divine aseity. It should be no surprise then that I reject the part-priority principle when it comes to substances. For substances, including

---

90. We could cite other examples too as reasons to reject the key premise. For example, consider a triangle. A triangle is a composite, composed of three straight lines joined together to form a closed plane. Triangles are necessary beings (on a traditional view of mathematical objects). But if necessary beings are things that exist uncaused then we have an example of an uncaused composite object, contra Aquinas' claim that all composite things are contingent things.

91. Aquinas, *The Treatise on the Divine Nature*, 35.

the divine substance, God is a fundamental unity of parts, properties, and powers. God's parts and properties are metaphysically dependent on God but not vice-versa (metaphysical dependency is not *causal* or *counterfactual* dependency). Rather, as a fundamental whole, God's parts (say, his ideas and thoughts) and his properties (the property of *being omnipotent*, *being omniscient*, etc.) exist as constituents in God and are either caused (in the case of ideas and thoughts) or uncaused (in the case of God's essential properties). Since my neo-Aristotelian account of substances, including the divine substance, is consistent with the doctrine of aseity, and since protecting divine aseity is the chief motivation for endorsing the doctrine of simplicity (for Aquinas and others), my view is equally orthodox.[92]

Moreover, setting to one side the worry about divine aseity, I don't think there are any other good reasons to adopt the doctrine of divine simplicity and there are a number of reasons for rejecting it. The Bible doesn't explicitly teach the doctrine of divine simplicity. Nor does the Bible endorse things about God that entail or require the doctrine of divine simplicity. To say, as Jacobs does in a footnote, that Exodus 3:14 provides a reason in support of the metaphysical claim of "existence as essence" (51 fn 83) is to wrongly impose a philosophical and foreign conceptual system onto the text. At most, "I am" can plausibly be interpreted to mean that God necessarily exists, not that God is simple. Worse, doctrines that are explicitly taught or implied in Scripture seem to rule out divine simplicity. In particular, the doctrine of the Trinity seems to entail genuine dependency relations between divine persons, a point that Jacobs tacitly acknowledges when noting that the "Trinity refers to a single substance with three inherent relations" (p. 52).

There are additional philosophical reasons for doubting the plausibility of the doctrine of simplicity. To cite but one example, consider the truth "God is good." On the doctrine of divine simplicity, God—the divine substance—is the truthmaker for this simple sentence. But what, we may ask, plays the role of truthbearer? The options seem to be divine thoughts, divine ideas, Platonic propositions, or human beliefs.[93] But simplicity rules out a plurality of divine thoughts and divine ideas and aseity rules out independently existing Platonic propositions. It seems we are left with one option: the truthbearers for intrinsic divine predications such as "God is good" are human beliefs. This entails the rather odd consequence that prior

---

92. For more on the compatibility of what Gregory Fowler calls the doctrine of divine priority and the doctrine of divine aseity, see Fowler, "Simplicity of Priority?" 114–38.

93. The rest of this paragraph summarizes the argument made by Allen Gehring in "Truthkmaking, Truthbearers, and Divine Simplicity."

to humans there were no *truths* about God.[94] The problem generalizes: if the only truthbearers are human beliefs and since humans do not exist in every possible world, then there are no necessary truths. Additionally, even in this world and at this time, there are bits of reality in which there is no truth about it since there are no human beliefs about those bits of reality (e.g., truths about the mass and color of a rock on some distant undiscovered planet). Since there are necessary truths, truths about God, and truths about bits of reality now unknown to humans, human beliefs can't be the only truthbearers. This problem dissolves if there are pluralities of divine ideas or thoughts had by a necessarily existing God that play the truthbearing role. But if there are pluralities of divine ideas and thoughts, as my *MTA* endorses, then divine simplicity ought to be rejected.[95]

Universals

Jacobs claims to endorse moderate realism, the view that there are universals but that they only exist in concrete particulars; i.e., there are no unexemplified universals. One cost of this view, already noted in my lead essay, is the rejection of the axiom of localization. If we are to understand his moderate realism at face-value, i.e., that "universals refer to real similarities in things with differences subtracted" (p. 40), then Jacobs is committed to the bizarre claim that one and the same universal is multiply located at different places at the same time. If, however, we are to understand Jacobs' language about "abstraction" to entail that universals only exist in minds but not literally "in" things, then the view is no longer a realist view. For then, "universals" are abstract particulars such that the redness of a truck and ball do not share the same numerically identical property; the redness of the truck and the redness of the ball are instances or tropes of redness that exactly resemble. If so, the problem of explaining why things are the same goes unanswered.

Let's assume that Jacobs endorses moderate or immanent realism regarding universals. Why think universals only exist if exemplified by concrete particulars? Perhaps the worry is that if some properties exist in a Platonic heaven (as I allow) then they are uncreated, threatening divine aseity. I've already argued that Platonic properties need not be thought of

---

94. The claim isn't that God doesn't exist prior to humans, rather the claim is there are no *truths* about God's existence or nature prior to humans.

95. Although see Panchuk, "The Simplicity of Divine Ideas," for a helpful discussion of one possible way to reconcile divine simplicity with the reality of divine thought that I find somewhat plausible, even if it doesn't address directly the worry I raise above regarding truthbearers. For additional problems with the doctrine of divine simplicity, see Plantinga, *Does God Have a Nature?*

as independently existing beings, thus the conjunction of theism and Platonism regarding properties does not entail the falsity of divine aseity.

Additionally, there are good reasons to think that unexemplified properties exist. J. P. Moreland lists three reasons I take to be decisive.[96] First, there seem to be necessary truths involving universals (e.g., "necessarily, redness is a color") and these truths plausibly entail that universals are necessary beings that exist in all possible worlds, including worlds where there are no concrete particulars. Second, by reflecting on the phenomenon of change, we learn truths about universals best explained by transcendent realism. For example, an apple was once green, is now red, and will soon be brown. Reflecting on the nature of change in the apple over time helps us see that while the apple changes, properties do not. Greenness (or redness or brownness) remains the same even as the apple—the concrete particular—undergoes an accidental change by losing and taking on distinct properties at various times. This suggests that universals are eternal, unchanging, necessarily existing objects that transcend their instances. Third, it seems more plausible to think that universals exist unexemplified prior to their instantiation instead of thinking that they come into existence with the advent of their instances. For example, it seems better to hold that prior to humans, the property *being human* existed as an unexemplified universal instead of thinking that the property came into existence with the advent of the first human. (I admit this third reason is an appeal to intuition and will have variable force for others. I do claim Plantinga as an ally though.)[97]

The Human Person

Finally, Jacobs writes, "a person is a whole composed of substantial form (soul) and matter (body)" (p. 45). If the "is" here picks out identity, then this view runs into problems with respect to disembodied existence. If Paul is identical to his matter-form composite, then, strictly speaking, Paul no longer exists upon separation from his body at death. Paul's soul continues to exist, but not Paul. But then, it is not correct to say, as Jacobs does, that in the disembodied state "*he* [i.e., Paul] remains individual" and that "*he* [i.e., Paul] looks forward to the resurrection" (p. 53 italics added) for there is no person, just the immaterial part of a person that remains upon death.

96. Moreland, *Universals*, 131–34.
97. Plantinga, *The Nature of Necessity*, 169. Plantinga's comment is embedded in a discussion about whether properties could be created or not. He thinks they can't. I think they can. We both agree that "to suppose that although they exist now, there was a time at which they did not . . . seems clearly false."

It is better, as I argue in my lead essay, to distinguish two senses of "object" when explicating the metaphysics of human beings: object *qua* substance and object *qua* agent. The first sense picks out human beings categorically speaking; i.e., Paul is a substance. The second sense picks out a human being's identity; i.e., Paul is identical to his soul, a soul that normally has a body. Or as stated in my lead essay, Paul is a *bodily soul*.

2.3 IDEALISM RESPONSE—JAMES SPIEGEL

I found Timothy Jacobs' elucidation of Aristotelian-Thomistic metaphysics to be intriguing and faithful to the long tradition of this perspective, which warrants serious consideration for the Christian. I appreciate Jacobs' close analysis of hylomorphism and application of the doctrine to a variety of metaphysical concerns, from the question of universals to personal immortality. In what follows I will make some critical points pertaining to a few aspects of Jacobs' account.

As Jacobs explains, according to Aristotelian hylomorphism, forms are not distinct entities that exist in some abstract Platonic realm. Rather, forms are always embedded in particulars. Jacobs affirms Aristotle's doctrine of substance as follows:

> Since a substance is an individual thing as a subject, we can talk about *kinds* of substances, like Peter and his dog. "Human" is not an individual thing but a similarity between Peter and his mom. Aristotle called the individual thing a *primary substance* and its kind, *secondary substance*, also called essence, (human) nature, or species. In short, a primary substance is a thing, and a secondary substance is a universal. (p. 38)

Primary substances undergo various changes. Some of these are accidental (e.g., painting a house, losing my hair, etc.), while other changes are substantial, such as when dirt is transformed into oats, which is then (through eating) transformed into a boy. Jacobs notes that the Aristotelian term for what underlies all change is prime matter. Prime matter is "what persists through changing from being *this* to *that*. Since change requires a subject to persist before, during, and after change as the subject we say changed, prime matter persists through substantial change" (p. 38).

My first concern pertains to this conception of matter. What exactly *is* such matter? Is it perceivable or even conceivable in itself apart from an object's perceivable form (shape, size, color, texture, etc.)? If not, then why suppose any such unperceivable underlying matter exists? After all, given that God is sufficient to sustain the ideational forms that are apparent to our minds, what non-redundant purpose could such a material substratum possibly serve? But if matter is not conceivable in itself apart from the perceivable form, then what intelligible meaning can we attach to the concept? It seems, then, that from a Christian metaphysical perspective Aristotelian prime matter is either explanatorily redundant or else unintelligible. Either way, prime matter serves no purpose in a Christian metaphysics.

Let us turn now to Jacobs' account of universals. He asserts that "universals refer to real similarities in things with differences subtracted, but not as separately existing immaterial forms" (p. 40). There is a fundamental problem with this approach to universals as mere similarities between substances. Even the notion of a "similarity" between things presupposes a pre-perceptual understanding of *what counts* as a similarity, which is itself knowledge of a universal truth. In short, one must *begin* with ideas of universals. One cannot arrive at universals merely via experience of particulars. This fact suggests the transcendency of universals. Furthermore, Jacobs' rejection of transcendent universals does not give proper due to the Platonist argument from perfection, which says that an *a priori* understanding of universals is implied by the fact that we routinely make judgments about degrees of perfection (e.g., whether a given circle or legal judgment achieves perfection), and such judgments assume *a priori* concepts of perfection in the relevant domains—concepts that could never be arrived at empirically. Understanding of such concepts seems to demonstrate that knowledge of universals precedes knowledge of particulars. And one need not infer a distinct ontological realm of abstract objects to account for this (as Platonists like Gould do). The mind of God is sufficient to account for the transcendent existence of universals. Moreover, if we are made in God's image, as the Bible says we are, then it is reasonable to suppose that in creating us in his image, God endowed our minds with a basic awareness of universals. So the seemingly innate understanding of universals need not be taken to imply reincarnation or any other form of premortal existence.

Finally, consider Jacobs' view of the human soul, which aims to overcome the interaction problem that always plagues substance dualisms, such as those of Plato and Descartes. According to Jacobs, the person as a "whole is a substance and soul and body become elements of it" (p. 45). And in order to account for the persistence of the soul after death, Jacobs appeals to the Thomistic notion that the intellect, or rational soul, is immaterial and therefore incorruptible. Thus, when a person dies, "this [rational] part persists, leaving behind physical powers" (p. 53). There are problems with this account. First, if the body and soul are each distinct substances that together form a more unified substance, how is real wholeness or unity possible when these are such distinct substances? Secondly, how does this view not suffer the same interaction problem as Platonist and Cartesian substance dualism? After all, Jacobs' account, too, must somehow make sense of a supposed interaction between the radically distinct body and soul substances. Finally, if the soul is not separate from the body and "matter is always united to form," then how can the soul "persist" when a person dies, "leaving behind physical powers"?

These are just a few of my concerns and questions regarding Jacobs' Aristotelian-Thomistic perspective. Unless he can resolve these problems, I am not hopeful that his view can be regarded as coherent, much less recommended as a plausible Christian metaphysics.

2.4 POSTMODERNISM RESPONSE
—SAM WELBAUM

Timothy Jacobs' chapter on Aristotelian-Thomistic metaphysics is very well done, and one with which I am in strong agreement. While I am taking the postmodern perspective in this book, particularly in regards the subjective, I am very Thomistic related to the objective, and therefore see many areas of overlap in our views. The strong focus on the physical, the embodied nature of reality, and the manner in which identity and essence are determined in relation to a community or a plurality of entities are a few of the points that were at least implied in Jacobs' chapter, and I think they are a key to a Christian understanding of metaphysics.

In particular, there are two ideas that Jacobs noted that I think have strong resonance with my position. When discussing Aristotle's four causes, he notes that Plato stopped at form and matter, but Aristotle saw that agency and purpose are necessary to fully understand a thing. Here we see the import of the one who does an action, or the one who crafts and makes an item, and that the item has a reason that it was made. Heidegger notes that hammers only matter because we live in a world with nails, and wood, and houses. Hammers are made by someone so that they might be used to make places for people to live, or rest. A potato peeler is not merely a metal object, but it was made by a craftsman so that someone can peel potatoes so that her family can eat. The dynamic relationship of subjects is key to metaphysics.

Later, when discussing Thomas' epistemology, Jacobs emphasizes human finitude, or limitation. He notes that if a pupil were tinted red, it would see the world as red, and then references Aquinas' assertion that to the person with a fever, everything tastes bitter. Though not Jacobs' intention, this is in part a nod to the situatedness of human existence. My perception of the world is one that is framed by the limitations of my humanity, and my situatedness within the world. Obviously this situatedness does not speak to the way that the world is, but rather the way that *my* world is, or rather, the way that I perceive the world. These points emphasized, there are two areas where I disagree, need clarification, or perhaps need education.

Universals, Abstraction, and Nominalism

While discussing the problem of universals, Jacobs presents three possible solutions. His presentation of Platonism is clear and does justice to the position. However, the other two options seem a bit murky. Obviously, all four of us are under space constraints, so Jacobs was limited in what he could address, but I don't believe he did justice to either nominalism, or hylomorphism. His presentation of nominalism appears to frame it as haphazard and capricious. He is right to indicate that nominalism is focused on particulars. The whiteness that I see in a stone is not the same whiteness that I see in snow, or Luke Skywalker's robe. They each have their own particular whiteness. However, nominalism rests on similarities. Universals are ways that we speak of similarities between objects, but the similarity is located in the two objects, not in a shared universal property. William of Ockham, the chief medieval nominalist himself, affirmed that similarity is a real relation.[98] The fact that the nominalist can see three white objects and see that they are similar and different is problematic for Jacobs' question, "If universals only refer to individuals, then how do we group Lassie and Odie under 'dog' but leave out a horse?" (p. 40). We can do this by noting that Lassie, Odie, and Trigger all have some similarities, but Trigger has hooves, and the tem "dog" is not used to apply to hooved animals.

However, this understanding of nominalism makes Jacobs' Aristotle a nominalist it seems, since universals are merely similarities. While there are many who would paint Aristotle this way, I don't think that is Jacobs' intention. I wonder if his view it might be more correct to say that in nominalism, universals are how we speak of similarities, but our minds associate the similarities to create the concept (anticipating Hume), whereas in hylomorphism, universals are real things that we discover in substances. Both involve abstraction, but one abstraction is creation, the other discovery. In this mode of thinking hylomorphism is like Platonism in that universals are discovered, but unlike Platonism, universals cannot exist apart from the material that they form.

---

98. Elliot, "Nominalism," 345–46.

Reincarnation and the Soul

The only other issue that I had with Jacobs' presentation is a statement he makes about reincarnation. This statement appears to be a "throw away" line, and not central to the argument, so I don't want to pay it too much attention to it. However, when discussing the union of the body and the soul, Jacobs' writes, "The soul of Peter is the form of *his* body and not Paul's body, so he cannot reunite to any body but his. Otherwise there would be no problem with reincarnation" (p. 50). He goes on to say that reincarnation is not a problem for Platonic dualism, and rightly cites the *Phaedo*. I wonder though, is the issue with reincarnation the fact that my soul is the soul of my body, or that my soul is my soul, unchanged? Whereas traditional doctrines of reincarnation entail my soul being "reset" or augmented so that my "me-ness" is replaced, Jacobs is correct, there is no place for that. However, is that due to the fact that my soul is the soul of my body, or due to the fact that my soul is my soul?

It also seems that, given the prolonged nature of the world, at the resurrection, there will be bodies that share particles with other bodies and therefore the composition of some bodies will be different. At that point, I wonder if the soul, as the form of the body, makes the body the self by means of enforming? As I said though, a minor point, but one that I think is important when it comes to understanding the union of the body and the soul.

2.5 ARISTOTELIANISM REPLY— TIMOTHY L. JACOBS

I am encouraged and impressed by the decorum of my critics. This is a conversation among friends in amiability and good taste. We all seek faithful Christian witness. I particularly enjoy seeing how Aristotelian-Thomistic metaphysics influences the other views.

Prime Matter

Prime matter is not an easy matter to understand, but it matters when we are discussing matters of subject and predicate. It is not mass or raw material. It is like "the matter at hand," "What's the matter?" or "the *subject* at hand." Some Thomists replace "prime matter" with "first subject," to avoid confusion.[99] Just as a proposition needs a subject and predicate, an object

---

99. See Jensen, *The Human Person*.

does too. Predicates define what the subject is (see my discussion of the five predicables). One understands the subject-predicate structure as a universal formula, but "subjectness" and "predicateness" do not form a proposition. You need a particular subject and predicate.

I say, "That *thing* is a *grabin*, a winged quadrupedal lizard." I made it up. It then loses its wings and feet to turn into a snake. Nearby, another *grabin* disappears, and a snake appears. The first *thing* underwent substantial change, while the second was annihilated and replaced by a third, created *ex nihilo*. The difference between change and annihilation-creation is that change needs an underlying subject that persists through the change. The underlying subject is neither a *grabin* nor a snake because neither was present the whole time. When a subject is a real thing, it has predicates, so to refer to the underlying subject without predicates identifying it as a particular thing, we need a new pronoun. We could say *it*, but let us say the *first (prime) subject* or *the prime subject matter of our investigation*, or simply *prime matter*.

Spiegel asks whether prime matter is "perceivable or even conceivable in itself" (p. 58). I ask, can you perceive "subject" without properties, or can it exist without them? To define a subject would ascribe predicates. Substantial change *just is* the change of all predicates. Prime matter is not aether, spiritual material, or substance of any kind, for these are *things* with properties. We can consider predicates without subjects, like right-handed or tall. We can also consider *subject* without predicates. It is impossible for either to exist without the other, both in a proposition or in things (except God). Prime matter is not a *thing* existing by itself anymore than right-handedness is. I may imagine it as a translucent aetherial material, but this is a placeholder to aid thought, a pronoun used to think of properties. Since the subject of a proposition or thing (aka prime matter) can be potentially anything, it is the predicates, the forms, that make it actually something, thus they have a kind of potency-act relationship.

Universals

Welbaum's clarification on universals and nominalism is accurate. Ockham sees universals as created names *only* referring to individuals. Aristotle sees them as real discovered predicates explicitly *not* referring to individuals. I see many right-handed people, then abstract the similarity by subtracting differences (the individuals) to understand it *as universal* without reference to any individual. Universals (or forms) have two modes of existence, *in reality* or *in the mind*. A. Mauer says, "Ockham's criticism of [Thomism] does not come to grips with its metaphysical notions of a nature and its possible ways of existing."[100]

Gould says it is a "bizarre claim that one and the same universal is multiply located at different places at the same time." That is only a problem if universals are things, as in Platonism. Gould is wrong that in Aristotelianism "universals only exist in minds but not literally 'in' things," and "then the view is no longer a realist view." A universal exists in the mind *as universal* and in things *as particular*. Gould rightly says this means "the redness of a truck and a ball do not share the same numerically identical property." My health is not my wife's health. They are numerically distinct, but when I abstract the similarity, I do not think *health* is an immaterial object. Denying ghosts makes me *more* of a realist, not *less*, even though Aristotle is unfortunately categorized as a moderate realist. Gould says, "Perhaps the worry is that if some properties exist in a Platonic heaven (as I allow) then they are uncreated, threatening divine aseity" (p. 56). First, I do not worry that Platonic heaven is a threat. I simply do not have sufficient reason to postulate universals as immaterial objects when hylomorphism is sufficient and avoids the pitfalls of Platonism. Further, I only think universals are created insofar as God created right-handedness, though I would say it is uncreated insofar as he eternally thinks it.

Spiegel says, "Even the notion of a 'similarity' between things presupposes a pre-perceptual understanding of what counts as a similarity, which is itself knowledge of a universal truth." Pure Lockean *tabula rasa* is insufficient, but inherent in the power of reason are logic, induction, etc.[101] Contra Kant, categories are learned as reason processes observation. The breadmaker works, but only when you add ingredients. Spiegel says my "rejection of transcendent universals does not give proper due to the Platonist argument from perfection, which says that an *a priori* understanding of universals is implied by the fact that we routinely make judgments about degrees of perfection . . . , and such judgments assume *a priori* concepts of perfection in the relevant domains—concepts that could never be arrived at empirically" (p. 59). Perfection *is* learned empirically and often by *via negativa*. I observe many circles, subtract differences, and abstract the universal definition "a plane figure with all points equidistant from a center." I do not need to see a perfect circle to know what it is. Likewise, I observe human reason, appetite, and other powers, subtract differences and flaws, and judge their proper use as human perfection. As Aquinas says, man can know what perfection is generally without revelation but needs revelation to know what

---

100. Mauer, *The Philosophy of William of Ockham*, 80.
101. Aristotle, *Posterior Analytics* 2.19.

specifically fulfills it, namely union with God.[102] We need revelation because we do not have innate knowledge.[103] Spiegel says, "If we are made in God's image . . . God endowed our minds with a basic awareness of universals" (p. 59). We cannot say, "if we are made in God's image, then [insert any divine attribute]." *Imago dei* is having intelligence, and consequently moral responsibility.

Gould recounts three of J. P. Moreland's arguments that exemplified properties exist (see his critique). First, that redness is necessarily a color is true insofar as the predicate is contained (and known *a priori*) in the subject as genus (category) is understood in species, but that need not mean the subject itself necessarily exists. Necessary truths are known to God eternally, but that does not imply they are immaterial objects in Plato's heaven, nor are they innately known to humans. Second, an apple changes as its properties change, but subject and properties considered abstractly in themselves are unchanging because they are not individuated. Third, universals existing in God's mind eternally do not imply they are immaterial self-subsisting objects.

The Soul

Welbaum's clarification on reincarnation is well taken and mostly accurate. Spiegel says hylomorphism suffers from the interaction problem because "if the body and soul are each distinct substances which together form a more unified substance, how is real wholeness or unity possible when these are such distinct substances?" Hylomorphism explicitly denies this substance dualism, partially because it has an interaction problem. Two entities need a means of communication or connection to be a whole. In hylomorphism, the soul and body are not parts anymore than the life and body of an animal are two parts, though they are two aspects. The soul is not a ghost in a machine but the power of life in the body, its "form." The power of locomotion uses legs, the power of vegetation uses digestion, etc., and the power of reason uses the brain. Reason persists postmortem because it is the only power that does not *need* matter (see my core presentation).

Gould says the Thomistic soul cannot remain individuated postmortem. In hylomorphism, just as the redness-of-this-apple is individuated by this-apple, so too the soul is the form *of a particular body*. Redness becomes

---

102 See Aquinas, *Summa Theologica* I–II.1.7, 2.8, 3.8, 5.1–8, esp. 5.3 & 5.8.

103. Conscience (Romans 2:12–16) is not innate knowledge but a judgment of practical reason that applies general moral principles of the natural law to particular situations driven by the natural inclination of synderesis. See Aquinas, *Summa Theologica* I.79.12–13. See also *Quaestiones Disputatae de Veritate* 16–17.

universal when it is seen as a similarity among many particulars. Human nature can be abstracted in this way, but not individual souls.

Gould says Thomism has an identity problem. If the self is the whole soul-body composite, it loses identity when separated. This is why Platonism says only the soul is the self. Rather, it is Platonism that has the identity problem because substance dualism has no unity. Is the subject of predication the soul, body, or whole? If the whole, then the whole is the subject, substance, or self, not one part. Embodied mind/soul cannot be a separate subject/substance from the body, a fact even affirmed by Gould's Platonism ("bodily soul"), so he partially borrows Aristotelian hylomorphism to harmonize with the Bible. Aquinas says when we attribute an action to someone, we say it is the person who understands or acts, not just their soul or body, but their whole self.[104] If the self were just the soul, it would be a pilot, and the body would not be part of the self. If self is a whole while embodied (hylomorphism), then the disembodied soul is not incomplete and longs to be whole again (resurrection). If self is whole when disembodied (Platonism), then the body was a non-essential property, something extraneous. But it is clear from the Bible that humans are essentially material, which is why the disembodied state is a temporary, incomplete existence that longs for resurrection.[105]

Divine Simplicity

I am actually surprised that Gould denied divine simplicity since it is affirmed by Clement, Basil, Cyril, Augustine, Boethius, John Damascene, Dionysuis, Anselm, Aquinas, as well as the Belgic Confession, John Owen, Francis Turretin, Jonathan Edwards, Herman Bavink, and many others who are by no means exclusively Aristotelian.[106] Augustine says "God is truly and

---

104. Aquinas, *Summa Theologica* I.76.1. Aquinas says, "Of one thing there is but one substantial being. But the substantial form gives substantial being. Therefore of one thing there is but one substantial form. But the soul is the substantial form of man. Therefore it is impossible for there to be in man another substantial form besides the intellectual soul" (*Summa Theologica* I.76.4, s. c.).

105. "We shall certainly be united with him in a resurrection like his" (Romans 6:5; cf. 1 Corinthians 15). See also Philippians 3:10–11; Revelation 20:5–6. Paul's reference to the body as a tent is not meant to see the body as a machine and the soul as a motor but to contrast mortal life with immortal life in union with Christ (2 Corinthians 5:1–10). Paul explicitly says humans do not have "heavenly bodies" but "earthly" bodies that are proper to what it is to be human (1 Corinthians 15:39–41).

106. Non-Christian defendants include Plato, Aristotle, Plotinus, Proclus, Avicenna, Averroes, Moses Maimonides. Before Christ, Jewish theologian Philo of Alexandria said that divine simplicity was already commonly accepted.

absolutely simple."[107] Nicholas Wolterstorff says divine simplicity is the ontological basis we have to "grant a large number of other divine attributes," and "one's interpretation of all God's other attributes will have to be formed in light of that conviction."[108] Richard Muller says "The doctrine of divine simplicity is among the normative assumptions of theology from the time of the church fathers, to the age of the great medieval scholastic systems, to the era of Reformation and post-Reformation theology, and indeed on into the succeeding era of late orthodoxy and rationalism."[109] Historically and biblically, divine simplicity is essential for aseity and transcendence.[110] It is not a denial of the many facets of divine attributes but an affirmation that God is the only self-sufficient being. Appeal to authority is insufficient justification, but space limits my defense to narrowly Aristotelian doctrines, not broadly Christian ones. For a thorough historic, philosophical, and biblical defense, see James Dozel's *God without Parts*. Here are a few dense starting points for readers to investigate themselves.

The trinitarian formula that God is *one substance* is an affirmation of simplicity. To use the Trinity to defend anything else risks heresies. *Substance* is an Aristotelian term adopted by Nicea. For this subject/substance to exist *a se* (of itself), his existence must be of his essence. Aseity is the very reason to affirm simplicity. Aquinas says, "If the existence of a thing differs from its essence, this existence must be caused either by some exterior agent or by its essential properties."[111] He says neither is true of God because the former makes God a creation and the latter implies he creates itself. Secondly, if essence is thought of as that which potentially exists and the explanation of its existence explains its actuality, then God's existence must be inherent in his essence so as to remain actual, uncaused, and without unactualized potency. "In every composite there must be potentiality and actuality," Aquinas says. Thus God is not composite. Third, When something exists, it participates in being, but God's existence is self-sufficient, not participated. Therefore, he is his own existence, just as he is his own essence.

---

107. Aquinas, *Expositio super Boethium De Trinitate* iv.6.7

108. Wolterstorff, "Divine Simplicity," 531.

109. Muller, *Post-Reformation Reformed Dogmatics*, Vol. III, 39.

110. Similar to doctrines like the Trinity, divine aseity, omnipresence, providence, immutability, self-sufficiency, and other divine attributes, a biblical defense will involve systematic and philosophical thinking. Divine simplicity is built on these doctrines and such passages as Malachi 3:6; James 1:17; Numbers 23:19; Exodus 3:14; Deuteronomy 6:4.

111. Aquinas, *Summa Theologica*, I–II.3.4. See also Aquinas, *Summa Contra Gentiles* I.31, especially on how the plurality of divine names (attributes) are not opposed to divine simplicity.

For Further Reading

Christian Aristotelian-Thomistic philosophy is prevalent through church history, and you can see how advocates of other views borrow from it. To learn more, refer to the books I cite. In particular, Feser is approachable and incorporates modern science while John Wippel provides an exhaustive Thomistic metaphysics.[112] Check out the Davenant Institute's *Natural Law* guidebook and their other publications and classes that recover historic Protestant thought.[113] For Thomistic body-soul psychology and ethics, see Steven Jensen.[114] C. S. Lewis' *Mere Christianity* provides an easy introduction to Thomistic ethics. You can also follow me at www.tljacobs.com. I welcome questions and continued dialogue.

BIBLIOGRAPHY

Aquinas, Thomas. *Commentary on Aristotle's De Anima: Sentencia libri De anima*. Translated by Kenelm Foster and Sylvester Humphries. New Haven, CT: Yale University Press, 1951.

———. *De Ente et Essentia*. Translated by Armand Mauer. 2nd rev. ed. Toronto: The Pontifical Institute of Mediaeval Studies, 1968.

———. *Expositio super Boethium De Trinitate*. Translated by Rose E. Brennan and Armand Mauer, 1953. Isidore, https://isidore.co/aquinas/BoethiusDeTr.htm.

———. *Quaestiones Disputatae de Anima*, translated by John Patrick Rowan. St. Louis: Herder, 1949.

———. *quaestiones Disputatae de Veritate*, edited by Joseph Kenny. Chicago: Regnery, 1954.

———. *Summa Contra Gentiles*. Edited by Joseph Kenny. New York: Hanover House, 1957.

———. *Summa Theologica*. Translated by the Fathers of the English Dominican Province. New York: Benzinger, 1948.

———. *The Treatise on the Divine Nature: Summa Theologiae I 1-13*. Translated by Brian J. Shanley, O.P. Indianapolis, IN: Hackett, 2006.

Aristotle. *Categories*. In *The Complete Works of Aristotle*, edited by Jonathan Barnes. 2 vols. Princeton, NJ: Princeton University Press, 1984.

———. *De Anima*. In *The Complete Works of Aristotle*, edited by Jonathan Barnes. 2 vols. Princeton, NJ: Princeton University Press, 1984.

———. *De Caelo*. In *The Complete Works of Aristotle*, edited by Jonathan Barnes. 2 vols. Princeton, NJ: Princeton University Press, 1984.

---

112. See Feser, *Scholastic Metaphysics*, *Aristotle's Revenge*, and *Five Proofs for the Existence of God*. See Wippel, *The Metaphysical Thought of Thomas Aquinas*.

113. See Haines and Fulford, *Natural Law*. See more at https://davenantinstitute.org/.

114. See Jensen, *The Human Person*, *Knowing the Natural Law*, and *Living the Good Life*.

———. *Metaphysics*. In *The Complete Works of Aristotle,* edited by Jonathan Barnes. 2 vols. Princeton, NJ: Princeton University Press, 1984.
———. *Nicomachean Ethics*. In *The Complete Works of Aristotle,* edited by Jonathan Barnes. 2 vols. Princeton, NJ: Princeton University Press, 1984.
———. *Physics*. In *The Complete Works of Aristotle,* edited by Jonathan Barnes. 2 vols. Princeton, NJ: Princeton University Press, 1984.
———. *Politics*. In *The Complete Works of Aristotle,* edited by Jonathan Barnes. 2 vols. Princeton, NJ: Princeton University Press, 1984.
———. *Posterior Analytics*. In *The Complete Works of Aristotle,* edited by Jonathan Barnes. 2 vols. Princeton, NJ: Princeton University Press, 1984.
———. *Protrepticus*. In *The Complete Works of Aristotle,* edited by Jonathan Barnes. 2 vols. Princeton, NJ: Princeton University Press, 1984.
Barr, Stephen. *Modern Physics and Ancient Faith*. Notre Dame, IN: University of Notre Dame Press, 2003.
Bradshaw, David. *Aristotle East and West: Metaphysics and the Division of Christendom*. Cambridge: Cambridge University Press, 2004.
Descartes, René. *Meditations*. Translated by John Veitch. London: Happy Reader, 2018.
Decaen, Christopher. "Elemental Virtual Presence in St. Thomas." *The Thomist* 64 (2000), 271–300.
Clarke, W. Norris. *The One and Many: A Contemporary Thomistic Metaphysics*. Notre Dame, IN: University of Notre Dame Press, 2014.
Dolezal, James. *God without Parts*. Eugene, OR: Pickwick, 2011.
Elliot, Mark. "Nominalism." In *The Cambridge Dictionary of Christian Theology,* edited by Ian A. McFarland et al., 345–46. Cambridge: Cambridge University Press, 2011.
Feser, Edward. *Aristotle's Revenge: The Metaphysical Foundations of Physical and Biological Science*. Heusenstamm, Germany: Editiones Scholasticae, 2019.
———. *Five Proofs for the Existence of God*. San Francisco: Ignatius, 2017.
———. *Scholastic Metaphysics: A Contemporary Introduction*. Heusenstamm, Germany: Editiones Scholasticae, 2014.
Fowler, Gregory. "Simplicity of Priority?" In *Oxford Studies in Philosophy of Religion,* edited by Jonathan Kvanvig, 114–38. Oxford: Oxford University Press, 2015.
Gehring, Allen. "Truthmaking, Truthbearers, and Divine Simplicity." *Philosophia Christi* 16.2 (2014) 297–317.
Haines, David, and Andrew Fulford. *Natural Law: A Brief Introduction and Biblical Defense*. Landrum, SC: The Davenant Trust, 2017.
Houser, Rollin. "Essence and Existence in Ibn Sīnā." In *The Routledge Companion to Islamic Philosophy,* edited by. Richard C. Taylor and Luis Xavier López-Farjeat, 212–24. London: Routledge, 2016.
———. *Logic as a Liberal Art: An Introduction to Rhetoric & Reasoning*. Washington, DC: The Catholic University of America Press, 2020.
Jacobs, Timothy. "Virtue/Vice Lists." In *Lexham Bible Dictionary,* edited by John D. Barry, n.p. Bellingham, WA: Lexham, 2014.
Jensen, Steven. *The Human Person: A Beginner's Thomistic Psychology*. Washington, DC: The Catholic University of America Press, 2018.
———. *Knowing the Natural Law: From Precepts and Inclinations to Deriving Oughts*. Washington, DC: The Catholic University of America Press, 2015.
———. *Living the Good Life: A Beginner's Thomistic Ethics*. Washington, DC: The Catholic University of America Press, 2013.

Kenny, Anthony. *Wittgenstein*. Oxford, Blackwell, 2006.

Kreeft, Peter. *Socratic Logic: A Logic Text using Socratic Method, Platonic Questions, and Aristotelian Principles*. Edition 3.1. South Bend, IN: St. Augustine, 2010.

MacIntyre, Alasdair. *After Virtue*. 3rd ed. Notre Dame, IN: University of Notre Dame, 2007.

Mauer, Armand. *The Philosophy of William of Ockham*. Toronto: Pontifical Institute of Mediaeval Studies, 1999.

Moreland, J. P. *Universals*. Montreal: McGill-Queen's University Press, 2000.

Muller Richard. *Post-Reformation Reformed Dogmatics*, Vol. III. Grand Rapids: Baker, 2003.

Panchuk, Michell. "The Simplicity of Divine Ideas: Theistic Conceptual Realism and the Doctrine of Divine Simplicity." *Religious Studies* 57.3 (2021) 385–402.

Plantinga, Alvin. *Does God Have a Nature?* Milwaukee, WI: Marquette University Press, 1980.

―――. *The Nature of Necessity*. Oxford: Oxford University Press, 1974.

Porphyry. *Introduction*: *Isagoge*. Translated by Jonathan Barnes. Oxford: Oxford University Press, 2003.

Plato. *Phaedo*. In *Plato: Complete Works*, edited by John M. Cooper. Indianapolis, IN: Hackett, 1997.

Wallace, William. *The Modeling of Nature: The Philosophy of Science and the Philosophy of Nature in Synthesis*. Washington, DC: Catholic University of America Press, 1996.

Wippel, John F. *The Metaphysical Thought of Thomas Aquinas: From Finite Being to Uncreated Being*. Washington, DC: Catholic University of America Press, 2000.

Wolterstoff, Nicholas. "Divine Simplicity." In *Philosophical Perspectives 5: Philosophy of Religion (1991)*, edited by James Tomberlin, 531–52. Atascadero, CA: Ridgefield, 1991.

3

Christian Metaphysics and Idealism

3.1 Idealism—James S. Spiegel
3.2 Platonism Response—Paul M. Gould
3.3 Aristotelianism Response—Timothy L. Jacobs
3.4 Postmodernism Response—Sam Welbaum
3.5 Idealism Reply—James S. Spiegel

3.1 IDEALISM—JAMES S. SPIEGEL

Introduction

As originally defined by Aristotle, metaphysics concerns "being as such"—what is most real. Although the set of specific issues that philosophers place in this category has expanded since the ancient Greeks, metaphysics still generally concerns what we might call fundamental reality. Today standard metaphysical issues include the nature of substance, properties, universals, time, space, causality, personal identity, and freedom. The metaphysician asks, what does it mean to say something exists? What is it to be a substance, a specific thing, or a certain kind of thing? What is the relation between a substance and its properties? What is a property? Are there universal properties such as "green" or "intelligent" which are shared by different substances? Or are there only particular things? What kind of substance or thing is a human being? What is the soul? Is it a separate substance or a property or set of properties of a physical body? What is God? And what is the relationship between God and all of these other things—physical substances, universals, and souls? These are all metaphysical questions, each of which I will address, and in the course of doing so I will present and defend an idealist metaphysical perspective.

In defending metaphysical idealism, I aim to do so in a distinctively Christian way. But now what does it mean to do metaphysics *Christianly*? In short, I would say a Christian metaphysics should be logically rigorous, empirically adequate, and theologically informed. With regard to the first point about logical rigor, as in any other domain of philosophical inquiry,

Christians should do metaphysics according to the received analytical standards of the field—using close analysis of concepts and arguments, appealing both to *a priori* and *a posteriori* evidence to support or challenge views under consideration. As to empirical adequacy, a Christian metaphysics should be reasonably informed, though not entirely constrained, by the most reliable findings of science and other empirical considerations. Thus, a reasonable metaphysical perspective should not blatantly contradict what we seem to know from the fields of physics and chemistry. And, thirdly, a Christian metaphysics must always proceed within the bounds of biblical authority. This might take one of two forms. At the least, the Christian metaphysician should consult Scripture as a filter or check on the results of their philosophical inquiry. But they may also conduct their metaphysical inquiry in such a way as to substantively inform their analyses of various concepts, problems, and arguments with biblical teachings about God, human nature, and the cosmos. This way of doing metaphysics is more in the style of philosophical theology.

The Nature of Existence

Idealism is a general term for the view that ideas and the minds that perceive them are what is most real. Philosophers from Plato to Augustine to Kant and Hegel are properly construed as idealists in an important sense. But the kind of idealism with which I am concerned is that affirmed by George Berkeley and Jonathan Edwards: that the entire physical world is mind-dependent. As Berkeley famously put it, *to be is to be perceived or to be a perceiver*.[1] So I will explicate Berkeley's brand of idealism here, as what I, and many other contemporary Christian philosophers, regard as the best version of the idealist thesis, considered both philosophically and theologically.

Berkeley's view is alternately dubbed "idealism" and "immaterialism." The terms are equally appropriate, though the latter is preferred by many because it is less ambiguous since, as just noted, thinkers ranging from Plato

---

1. Here I will focus on Berkeley's defense of metaphysical idealism since it is far more extensively developed and historically influential than that of Edwards. But Edwards' commitment to the idealist thesis is unequivocal. In his early essay "Of Being," he asserts, "nothing has any existence anywhere else ... but either in created or uncreated consciousness." In "Miscellany 179" he declares that "the existence of all corporeal things is only ideas." And late in his career, in his "Notes on Knowledge and Existence," Edwards says, "there is no such thing as material substance truly and properly distinct from all those that are called sensible qualities, ... a body is nothing but a particular mode of perception." See Edwards, *The Works of Jonathan Edwards*, 6:55–136, 13:327, and 6:398, respectively.

to Hegel are called "idealists." The essential difference between the terms is that "idealism," in the Berkeleyan sense, is a positive term, asserting that all that is real are ideas existing in minds. In contrast, "immaterialism" is a negative term, denying that matter is real. But it is crucial to understand exactly what sense of matter Berkeley's thesis denies. Berkeley does not deny the existence of ordinary physical objects we encounter everywhere we go. Rather, he denies the existence of matter in the sense affirmed by the early modern philosopher John Locke. According to Locke, the sensible qualities that we perceive in an object must subsist or inhere in some sort of underlying stuff or material "substratum" which is itself unperceivable.[2] It is this substratum that underlies, say, the redness, solidity, smoothness, sweetness, and crunchiness of the apple on my desk. It is not just a collection of qualities. Locke recognizes that material substance is itself unperceivable and even grants that we cannot even form an idea of it, calling it "we know not what."[3] But he insists that such substratum must exist in order to causally explain the unity and stability of the qualities of physical objects.

So why would Berkeley deny the existence of material substance? One of Berkeley's answers to this question is that we have no positive reason to affirm its existence. For one thing, no one has ever perceived material substratum, nor, as Locke himself admits, can we even conceive it in our minds. So the concept of matter is unintelligible. As Berkeley puts it, "the very notion of what is called *matter* or *corporeal substance* involves a contradiction."[4] As for Locke's causal argument, this is a spurious justification for anyone who is a theist. Why posit the existence of an unthinking, unperceivable, inconceivable substratum to explain the unity and stability of physical objects when an almighty God is more than sufficient to account for this? So on a theistic worldview, material substratum is ontologically redundant. To posit the existence of material substance violates Ockham's razor, the principle of parsimony, which says that, other things being equal, the simpler of two explanations is to be preferred.[5]

---

2. Locke writes, "not imagining how . . . *ideas* can subsist by themselves, we accustom ourselves, to suppose some *substratum*, wherein they do subsist, and from which they do result, which therefore we call *substance*." Locke, *An Essay Concerning Human Understanding*, 295.

3. As Locke puts it, "if anyone will examine himself concerning his *notion of pure substance in general*, he will find he has no other *idea* of it at all, but only a supposition of he knows not what support of such qualities, which are capable of producing simple *Ideas* in us." Locke, *An Essay Concerning Human Understanding*, 295.

4. Berkeley, *The Principles of Human Knowledge*, section 9.

5. For some helpful discussions of this principle, see Smart, "Ockham's Razor," 118–28, and Walsh, "Occam's Razor: A Principle of Intellectual Elegance," 241–44.

This line of argument helps us to see why Berkeley is properly called an "immaterialist," since his thesis is essentially that material substratum does not exist. But Berkeley's core argument shows why the positive appellation of "idealist" is just as appropriate. When we examine that apple on my desk, or any other physical object, what we encounter is a collection of sensible qualities—in this case, again, redness, smoothness, sweetness, crunchiness, etc. What are these qualities but *ideas*? And ideas, of course, are properly understood to be whatever is present to the mind when one thinks, reflects, or perceives. Ideas are, by definition, mind-dependent things. They do not exist on their own but only in the minds that conceive them. Now no matter how closely we analyze the apple we never discover anything except more sensible qualities or ideas. So if physical objects such as apples are nothing but collections of ideas, and ideas are by definition mind-dependent, it follows that the entire physical world is mind-dependent. Berkeley's conclusion, then, is that all that exist are ideas and the minds that perceive them, which is the idealist thesis. Therefore, whether we call Berkeley an immaterialist or an idealist, it amounts to the same thing. These two terms simply express his thesis in negative or positive terms, respectively.

Berkeley supplements his argument for the idealist thesis with an appeal to perceptual relativity. The qualities of objects that we perceive with our senses vary with context and circumstance. Depending upon one's position or point of view, a given object may appear larger or smaller. An article of clothing may appear to be brown or dark green depending upon lighting. Orange juice may taste sweet or sour, depending on whether one has just eaten buttered toast or a peppermint candy. Indeed, every quality possessed by a physical object may be construed differently by different people or by the same person in different circumstances.[6] Such perceptual relativity strongly suggests mind-dependence of physical objects, according to Berkeley.

Berkeley's arguments can be reinforced with some arguments from science and Scripture. As the eminent philosopher of science Karl Popper observed, Berkeley actually anticipated Einsteinian relativity theory, among other developments in twentieth-century physics.[7] Berkeley was considered radical in his time for questioning the commonly accepted Newtonian notion of absolute time, space, and motion. But Einstein's theory of special relativity sparked a revolution in physics, according to which we now recognize a linkage between space, time, and motion. These are relative, not absolute, physical realities. And later, with the advent of quantum physics, emerged an

---

6. Berkeley makes this argument in *The Principles of Human Knowledge*, sects. 14–15 and *Three Dialogues between Hylas and Philonous*, first dialogue.

7. Popper, *Conjectures and Refutations*, chapter 6.

even more significant confirmation of Berkeley's thesis. Specifically, quantum events are observer-dependent. According to the Copenhagen interpretation, advanced by Niels Bohr and Werner Heisenberg, a physical system cannot be said to have any definite properties until it is observed.[8] This account of the implications of quantum mechanics remains a standard one, bizarre and surprising as it might appear. But it would have appeared neither bizarre nor surprising to Berkeley, whose philosophical insights led him to the same conclusion two centuries prior to the work of these scientists.

Finally, consider the biblical argument for idealism, which is fairly straightforward. First, Scripture teaches that all things depend for their existence upon God, who constantly sustains the universe. In the book of Acts, the apostle Paul asserts that in God "we live and move and have our being" (Acts 17:28).[9] And the writer of Hebrews declares that God "sustain[s] all things by his powerful word" (Hebrews 1:3). This is the doctrine of divine conservation, which is essentially an extension of the doctrine of divine creation *ex nihilo*—the notion that God created all things purely and simply, without the use of any pre-existing stuff. The doctrine of divine conservation affirms that the continuation of the physical universe is no less an active work of God than the original cosmic creative act. Secondly, Scripture teaches that God is a mind or spirit (e.g., John 4:24 and innumerable other passages), which is to say that God is a center of consciousness, presumably—given the doctrine of *imago Dei*—in some way similar to the way human beings are centers of consciousness. Now combining these two biblical teachings—the doctrine of divine conservation and that God is mind—we can only conclude that the physical world is mind-dependent, which is essentially the idealist thesis.

Universals

Having summarized the main arguments for Berkeleyan idealism, let's apply this thesis to basic metaphysical issues, beginning with the question of universals. Generally speaking, a universal is an entity or property that can be multiply instantiated, that is, realized in many distinct objects. Thus, the universals featured in my apple are the properties of redness, roundness, smoothness, sweetness, and crunchiness. Each of these attributes are found in many other objects. Cars and doors are sometimes red. Basketballs and

---

8. See Heisenberg, *Physics and Philosophy*; Mohanty, "Idealism and the Quantum Mechanics"; Wimmel, *Quantum Physics & Observed Reality*; Folger, "Does the Universe Exist if We're Not Looking?"

9. All biblical quotes are taken from the *New International Version of the Bible*.

balloons may be round. And so it goes for smoothness, sweetness, and crunchiness. All of these properties are instantiated in countless other objects besides this apple. One might say that all physical objects are similarly combinations of such universals, since every quality of every physical object is also a property of some other physical object. However, universals are not limited to sensible qualities such as colors, shapes, and tastes. Abstract properties such as love, justice, and beauty are also universals, since these, too, are multiply instantiated. But whether sensible or abstract, regarding any universal we seem to have general concepts of them.

So what is the ontological status of universals according to idealism? First, let's consider the three standard views on the issue. *Nominalists* deny the existence of universals, insisting that only particulars exists. Thus, says the nominalist, there is no such thing as general redness or justice. There is only this or that red car or ruby and only this or that just person or policy. Although we use general terms like redness and justice, these are merely names for realities that exist only and always as particulars. According to nominalism, universals exist in name only. All that exist are particulars.[10]

Realism is the view that universals are mind-independent entities. There is a range of realist perspectives. Plato maintained that universals, or "forms," have an immutable, eternal, abstract existence, and particular objects and properties, such as apples, redness, and justice, exemplify these abstract realities. The particular objects and properties we experience in this world are, at best, poor imitations of the perfect eternal forms. Aristotle, too, was a realist about universals, but he denied that they exist independently of the objects in which they are instantiated. Universals exist, he maintained, only when they are exemplified and exist, as it were, as the property that is common to their various instantiations. The debate between Platonist and Aristotelian realists regarding whether universals may exist independently of physical exemplification has persisted for over two millennia. But they and all other realists agree that universals are mind-independent.

Finally, *conceptualists* maintain that universals exist as concepts in minds. Historically, conceptualists have been seen as occupying a middle position between nominalism and realism, affirming the reality of universals but denying that this reality is extra-mental. Importantly, two forms of conceptualism may be distinguished, depending upon whether universals are taken to exist just in human minds or ultimately in the mind of God. We might call these two views, respectively, *subjective* and *theistic*

---

10. Prominent nominalists include David Hume, W. V. O. Quine, and Wilfrid Sellars.

conceptualism. In the spectrum of views on universals, the former view is much closer to nominalism, while the latter is closer to realism.[11]

Having distinguished the major views on universals, we may now answer the question regarding the idealist perspective on the issue. As it turns out, idealists have some options here. They may affirm nominalism or conceptualism. Only realism seems out of consideration, because idealists believe that all non-minds are mind-dependent. Berkeley scholars have disagreed over whether Berkeley was himself a nominalist or conceptualist. To complicate matters further, the later Berkeley actually appears to have been sympathetic with Platonism.[12] But which view is the *best fit* with an idealist metaphysics? In my view, idealism is most naturally allied with theistic conceptualism, where universals exist as archetypes in the mind of God. So understood, Berkeley's cozying up to Platonism toward the end of his career is understandable. The divine archetypes may be conceived along the lines of Platonic forms, though with the important qualification that they do not exist independently.

Particulars

All of this enables us to answer another related metaphysical question: What is a particular? What is the relation between a specific thing, such as an apple, and its various properties? Here, again, there are three major theories, one of which is ruled out by Berkeley's thesis. First, there is the Lockean *substratum theory*, which says a particular object is a material substratum which "supports" or "underlies" its properties. This additional underlying stuff is sometimes called a "bare particular." So, on this view, a given particular is a combination or fusion of a substratum and a set of properties.[13] Secondly, there is the *bundle theory*, according to which particular sensible objects are simply bundles of properties. There is nothing more nor less to a particular thing than all of its properties.[14] Thirdly, there is the Aristotelian

---

11. John Locke appears to have been a subjective conceptualist, while Thomas Aquinas was a theistic conceptualist, as I've defined these terms here.

12. Specifically, in Berkeley's *Siris*.

13. Proponents of the substratum theory include John Locke, *An Essay Concerning Human Understanding*, II.23 and the early Bertrand Russell, "On the Relations of Universals and Particulars." More recent advocates include Gustav Bergmann, *Realism*, and Ted Sider, "Bare Particulars."

14. The bundle theory was defended by the later Russell in *Inquiry into Meaning and Truth*, as well as Ayer in *Philosophical Essays*. Other advocates of the view include O'Leary-Hawthorne, "The Bundle Theory of Substance and the Identity of Indiscernibles," and Casullo, "Particulars, Substrata, and the Identity of Indiscernibles."

substance theory. On this view, particulars are not reducible to their component parts or properties but are fundamentally wholes that are greater than the sum of their parts. Substances include living things and so-called "material simples," such as atoms, which compose physical objects. Some scholars have suggested that the substance theory occupies a middle position between the substratum and bundle views.[15] Like the substratum theory, the substance view affirms that a particular object has properties but it denies that an unperceivable "bare particular" is the substrate of these properties. The bearer of the properties of a particular apple is not some unperceivable substrate but rather the apple itself. It is the *apple* that is red, round, smooth, sweet, and crunchy.

So what is the Berkeleyan idealist's account of particulars? Following Steven B. Cowan, I would say this depends on what kind of particular we are talking about.[16] When it comes to purely physical inanimate objects, such as footballs, cars, and apples, the bundle theory is the best account, since there is nothing more to sensible objects than the properties of which they are constituted. But living things are different, since they possess minds or souls. Accordingly, a human being (or a dog, monkey, whale, or anything else that has a perceiving mind) is a combination of an irreducible substance—that is, its soul—and the bundle of properties that constitute his or her perceivable, physical body.

This naturally raises the question, what *is* the soul? In the next section I will discuss the idealist view of the soul, but I would like to conclude this section with a summary elucidation of a Berkeleyan account of universals and particulars that reinforces the theistic foundation of idealism. In his remarkable apologetic work entitled *Alciphron*, Berkeley proposed that the physical world is quite literally a divine language, a system of visible signs by which God speaks, as it were, to our eyes:

> Upon the whole, it seems the proper objects of sight are light and colours, with their several shades and degrees; all which, being infinitely diversified and combined, form a language wonderfully adapted to suggest and exhibit to us the distances, figures, situations, dimensions, and various qualities of tangible objects: not by similitude, nor yet by inference of necessary connexion, but by the arbitrary imposition of Providence, just as words suggest the things signified by them.[17]

---

15. See, for example, Loux, *Metaphysics: A Contemporary Introduction*, 111.
16. Cowan, "What *Is* that Stone? Idealism and Particulars," 51–69.
17. Berkeley, *Alciphron*, 154.

Berkeley's account of the physical world as a sort of language here is no mere metaphor. After all, in any language there are certain signs—whether visible letters or audible sounds—which are used to suggest meanings to our minds. This is precisely what we encounter in the physical world—combinations of sensible qualities that also suggest meanings to the minds of human perceivers. Thus, as Berkeley puts it, "the great Mover and Author of Nature constantly explaineth Himself to the eyes of men by the sensible intervention of arbitrary signs." For this reason, he says, "you have as much reason to think the Universal Agent or God speaks to your eyes as you can have for thinking any particular person speaks to your ears."[18]

To unpack this idea a bit, consider the components of a written or spoken language. Every word is a distinct "particular" that conveys a specific meaning or idea, from one mind to another. And each particular word is composed of "universals." Thus, the particular word "apple" is comprised of the English language universals "a," "p," "p," "l," and "e." And the sentence "May I eat this apple?" consists of several words placed in an order that, according to the English rules of syntax, conveys a distinct meaning. Every word is analyzable into its component letters. Each sentence is analyzable into its component words. And highly complex and multifaceted meanings may emerge as words are arranged in various orders.

Now notice the parallels in the physical world, where each physical object, such as an apple, is composed of universals (i.e., red, round, smooth, sweet, crunchy, etc.). Here we have the essence of the Berkeleyan doctrine of particulars. A particular object just is a unique combination of universal qualities. Of course, for any given object, each of the universal qualities appears repeatedly in human experience, but no two particular objects are exactly the same because of the varying combinations, however slight, of the universals that compose different objects. (Even if two objects were exact replicas of one another, they would still be distinct in terms of their locations and proximities to other objects.) Furthermore, the rules of syntax of the divine visual language are what we call the laws of nature, which we must abide by in order to operate properly, provide explanations, and discern "meanings" in nature. Finally, just as whole novels can be constructed from particular words, and words from universal letters, the entire universe is built up from particular objects, and these objects from the universal sensible qualities that constitute them.

This linguistic analysis of the Berkeleyan account of the physical world is what Colin Turbayne calls Berkeley's "metaphysical grammar."[19] It not only

---

18. Berkeley, *Alciphron*, 157.
19. The foregoing analysis highlights some of the major elements of Turbayne's

illuminates an important aspect of the idealist conception of the relationship between universals and particulars, but it underscores the centrality of God in our understanding of the physical world. On the Berkeleyan view, just as linguistic partners are continually "decoding" one another's use of visible and audible "signs" in the form of written and oral communication, every human being is constantly decoding the divine signs of nature which constitute God's visual language. In fact, the physical world essentially is that system of linguistic signs through which minds interact—whether between created minds or between the divine mind and created minds.

The Human Soul

Now let us consider the place of the human soul in a Berkeleyan idealist metaphysics. For Berkeley, there are just two ontological categories: minds (or souls or spirits) and ideas. A mind is an active perceiving conscious substance, essentially a thinking thing. As Berkeley puts it, "the Mind, Spirit, or Soul is that indivisible unextended thing which thinks, acts, and perceives."[20] This is in deep contrast to ideas, which are wholly passive and unthinking.[21] In each of these two basic ontological categories, there are two subcategories. The two kinds of minds include finite, created minds (e.g., humans, angels, animals, etc.) and one infinite, divine mind—God. The two kinds of ideas are real and imaginary. Real ideas are the ordinary objects that comprise the physical world, accessed via sense experience. Imaginary ideas, on the other hand, are those concocted by our own minds.

While ideas are sensible or at least imaginable, minds/spirits are neither sensible nor imaginable: "a spirit [is] the only substance or support wherein the unthinking beings or ideas can exist; but that this substance which supports or perceives ideas should itself be an idea or like an idea is evidently absurd."[22] While it is impossible to form an idea of mind, Berkeley maintains we nonetheless may *know* minds, not via ideas but by what he calls "notions." He says, "We may not . . . be said to have an idea of an active being . . . , although we may be said to have a notion of them . . . ."[23]

---

insightful discussion. See Turbayne, "Berkeley's Metaphysical Grammar," 3–36.

20. George Berkeley, *Three Dialogues between Hylas and Philonous*, 92. See also Berkeley, *Principles of Human Knowledge*, sect. 93.

21. Berkeley writes, "all the unthinking objects of the mind agree in that they are entirely passive, and their existence consists only in being perceived; whereas a soul or spirit is an active being whose existence consists, not in being perceived, but in perceiving ideas and thinking," *Principles of Human Knowledge*, sect. 139.

22. Berkeley, *Principles of Human Knowledge*, sect. 135.

23. Berkeley, *Principles of Human Knowledge*, sect. 142.

Exactly what he means by this is difficult to discern.[24] However, it must be emphasized that this difficulty is not uniquely a problem for Berkeley or idealists more generally. It is a problem for all mind-body dualists and anyone else who believes that minds are distinct ontological entities.[25]

But, it is fair to ask, how do we *gain* this "notion" of spirits—whether human or divine? Berkeley's answer is that we acquire this through the ideas that spirits produce in us. Berkeley puts it like this:

> It is plain that we cannot know the existence of other spirits otherwise than by their operations, or the ideas by them excited in us. I perceive several motions, changes, and combinations of ideas that inform me there are certain particular agents, like myself, which accompany them and concur in their production. Hence, the knowledge I have of other spirits is not immediate, as is the knowledge of my ideas, but depending on the intervention of ideas, by me referred to agents or spirits distinct from myself, as effects or concomitant signs.[26]

Note how with this account Berkeley places on the same logical plane our means of knowing all spirits, whether human or divine. Just as God is known by reflecting about his works in nature, so human minds are similarly known in this indirect fashion. Because our encounters with fellow humans are so routine and their communications with us are less subtle, it is easy to overlook the fact that our knowledge of other human minds is, at best, indirect. In fact, the "problem" of other minds—the challenge of demonstrating that there are other minds besides your own—remains a perplexity in the field of philosophy, a problem that arguably is still unsolved. Perhaps our belief in other minds is actually a faith commitment. Thus, when it comes to our belief in other human minds, here is further reason to affirm epistemic parity with belief in God. For many evidential arguments have been put forth to justify belief in both the divine mind and other human minds, but also in both domains the arguments are controversial. This

---

24. See Ramsey, "Notions and Ideas in Berkeley's Philosophy," 66–71; Furlong, "Berkeley on Relations, Spirits, and Notions," 60–66; Cornman, "Theoretical Terms, Berkeleian Notions, and Minds," 161–81; and Woozley, "Berkeley's Doctrine of Notions and Theory of Meaning," 427–34.

25. Because minds, on the dualist view, are not tangible, visible, or sensible in any way, specifying precisely how they are comprehended or known is profoundly challenging, which is the basis of a long-standing physicalist objection to dualism. Of course, physicalists are arguably even worse off than dualists on this score, since they face the double problem of precisely characterizing how we know minds *and* how consciousness emerges from or is reducible to physical structures and processes.

26. Berkeley, *Principles of Human Understanding*, sect. 145.

further underscores the reasonableness of Berkeley's lumping knowledge of human and divine minds into the same epistemic category.

The Berkeleyan idealist regards the mind or spirit as the seat of personal identity. Berkeley says, "What I am myself, that which I denote by the term *I*, is the same with what is meant by *soul* or *spiritual substance*."[27] And our souls are made in the image of God.[28] So the Berkeleyan idealist is certainly a mind-body dualist, but it must be emphasized that this is *not* substance dualism. Recall that on the Berkeleyan view the only substances are spirits. Our bodies are collections of ideas, and ideas are not substances. This is not to say that our bodies, or any other physical entities, are any less real than our common sense would have us believe (a common misconception of Berkeley). Rather, it is just to say that bodies have no mind-independent reality. They exist only when perceived. Note here a major benefit of this view for thinking about philosophy of mind. Since the idealist brand of mind-body dualism affirms that only spirits are true substances, this view does not face the interaction problem that vexes all versions of substance dualism. For Cartesians and other substance dualists, there is pressure to account for how such radically different substances could causally interact. For Berkeleyan idealists there is no such problem, since only minds are substances and ideas are the natural currency of minds.

The Central Divine Reality

It should be clear from all that has been said that God is central to a Berkeleyan idealist metaphysics. Simply put, all that exists is God, his thoughts, and the finite spirits with whom he shares these thoughts. Demonstrating this was Berkeley's primary motive in defending his "*esse* is *percipi*" thesis. Hence, Berkeley concludes his *Principles of Human Knowledge* by noting that

> What deserves the first place in our studies is the consideration of God and our duty; which to promote, as it was the main drift and design of my labors, so shall I esteem them altogether useless and ineffectual if, by what I have said, I cannot inspire my readers with a pious sense of the presence of God . . . the better to dispose them to reverence and embrace the salutary truths of the Gospel, which to known and to practice is the highest perfection of human nature.[29]

27. Berkeley, *Principles*, sect. 139.

28. Berkeley writes, "I have . . . in myself some sort of active thinking image of the Deity." *Three Dialogues between Hylas and Philonous*, 93.

29. Berkeley, *Principles of Human Understanding*, sect. 156.

But exactly how does a Berkeleyan perspective enhance one's sense of the presence of God? Otherwise put, what is it about idealism that renders theism and the Christian gospel more reasonable? Elsewhere I have addressed this question in some depth, but here I will simply summarize some of the more significant ways that idealism reinforces a Christian perspective.[30] First, given idealism, *the evidence for God is ubiquitous.* If each of the physical objects around us, indeed the entire physical universe, is mind-dependent, and we know that these objects do not depend upon our own minds, so they must exist only because the infinite mind is perceiving them. And since ideas cannot exist on their own, the divine activity that produced the physical world cannot have been a singular act in the distant past but rather must be a continuing work of God to sustain everything in being. So the present reality of God is evident literally everywhere one looks. This is a profound boon to faith and, as was Berkeley's intention, it leaves no room for atheism, agnosticism, or religious skepticism.[31]

A second way in which idealism reinforces a theistic perspective regards theoretical parsimony. According to the principle popularly known as "Ockham's razor," we should grant preference to those theories that are most simple or elegant. That is, other things being equal, we should prefer theoretical perspectives that use the fewest entities or principles to explain the relevant data. So how does the idealist ontology fare on this standard? A Lockean "matterist" ontology posits the existence of two kinds of substances—matter and mind. But Berkeleyan idealism affirms only one kind of substance—mind. This is obviously more parsimonious and thus preferable, other things being equal, to matterism. Furthermore, idealism enables the theist to rebut a long-standing objection by naturalists who tout the parsimony of their ontology, which affirms materialist monism. Idealism, as it turns out, is just as parsimonious as naturalism. However, unlike naturalism, idealism provides a ready explanation for many natural facts about the world that are inexplicable on a naturalist perspective, including the origin of the universe, the emergence of life, biological fine-tuning, and the emergence of consciousness.[32] So, again, idealism greatly enhances the reasonableness of theism.

---

30. See Spiegel, "Idealism and the Reasonableness of Theistic Belief," 11–28.

31. Regarding this and a variety of related points, see Hight, "How Immaterialism Can Save Your Soul," 109–22.

32. Furthermore, idealism arguably *avoids* all of the problems of consciousness that plague materialist accounts of the mind, such as awareness, perception, intentionality, subjectivity, qualia, and freedom. For a discussion of some of these points, see Taliaferro, "Idealism and the Mind-Body Problem," 91–106.

Thirdly, idealism provides a satisfying account of natural laws and miracles. Among the challenges in philosophy of science is explaining the various regularities in nature that are called "laws of nature," including the inverse square law, Avogadro's constant, the laws of thermodynamics, Boyle's law, and numerous other regularities in physics and chemistry. An associated problem in philosophy of religion regards how to make sense of how these laws are apparently violated or suspended in the event of miraculous events, such as Jesus' walking on water or instantly healing a leper. On a Berkeleyan idealist perspective, both of these things are accounted for in the same way—by appealing to immediate divine governance of the physical world. Berkeley writes,

> the set rules or established methods wherein the mind we depend on excites in us the ideas of sense are called the laws of nature; and these we learn by experience, which teaches us that such and such ideas are attended with such and such other ideas in the ordinary course of things.[33]

God arranges such cosmic regularities both to ensure that our planet is hospitable to life and to benefit us with the foresight they provide with regard to what sorts of actions lead to which sorts of consequences, thus enabling human beings to plant, harvest, build, keep warm, and generally flourish. However, since these regularities are ordained by God, he can also arrange for exceptions to them for good purposes. As Berkeley puts it, "The Author of Nature [may] display His overruling power in producing some appearance out of the ordinary series of things. Such exceptions from the general rules of nature are proper to surprise and awe men into an acknowledgment of the Divine Being."[34] And these exceptions are what we call miracles, which are simply purposeful, redemptive exceptions to God's routine manner of governing the cosmos.

Berkeleyan idealism easily accounts for both natural laws and the occurrence of miracles. This is because the physical world just is God's public ideas, and God has complete control over all of his ideas. Thus, it is evident that idealism commits one to a strong view of divine providence. It also has implications for how one conceives of the relationship between human and divine agency. When it comes to this issue, there are three major perspectives: mere conservationism, occasionalism, and concurrentism. According to *mere conservationists* God does not act directly in the world; rather his causal impact on physical events is indirect and remote. When I choose

---

33. Berkeley, *Principles of Human Understanding*, sect. 30.
34. Berkeley, *Principles of Human Understanding*, sect. 63.

to pick up my apple to take a bite, it is I alone who is moving my arm. God merely sustains the apple and me in being, enabling me to perform such acts. The mere conservationist view thus minimizes the role of divine agency in the world while maximizing the role of creaturely agency. *Occasionalists* reverse this emphasis, insisting that all physical events are divinely dictated and that creatures play no actual causal role. Thus, when I pick up the apple and take a bite, it is God who moves my arm and my mouth. My own mind's decision was merely the "occasion" on which God arranged the movement of my body according to my voluntary choice. And so it goes for all human activity. There is no real creaturely agency on this view. Finally, *concurrentists* aim to strike a middle position between mere conservationism and occasonalism, affirming the reality of both divine and human agency. With the occasionalist, they say that God is causally active in all natural events, including free human choices. And with the mere conservationist, they affirm that human beings possess causal powers and genuinely act in the world. So when I pick up and bite the apple, this movement is caused by both God and me. I voluntarily act, and God concurs in producing the event.[35]

To which of these views is the Berkeleyan idealist committed? Clearly, she must eschew mere conservationism, since this view rejects the core idealist claim that God is the immediate cause of all of the phenomena of nature. So that leaves occasionalism and concurrentism. As it turns out, there has been much scholarly debate over whether Berkeley himself was an occasionalist or a concurrentist. A careful review of the Berkeley corpus suggests that he was either undecided or confused on the issue, as there is textual evidence to support either interpretation of Berkeley. But which view of divine and human agency *should* a Berkeleyan idealist embrace? That is, which view *fits best* with a Berkeleyan idealist metaphysic? I am inclined to say that a concurrentist perspective makes the most sense, all things considered, from the standpoint of Berkeleyan idealism.[36] But for our purposes here, I would grant that an idealist may opt to affirm either occasionalism or concurrentism. Both are viable options when it comes to the issue of divine and human agency.

---

35. These are rough summaries of these views. For in-depth discussions of each, see Morris, *Divine and Human Action*.

36. For an extensive discussion of this issue and defense of this interpretation, see Spiegel, "Berkeley on Divine and Human Agency."

Conclusion

To conclude, it will be helpful to summarize the Berkeleyan idealist view by applying it to some concrete cases. So, on the idealist perspective, what does it mean to say that God created Peter and Paul as human beings made in God's image who came into existence, died, and will be resurrected from the dead?

Generally speaking, the idealist affirms that Peter and Paul are divine creations who bear the image of God and are sustained in existence by God from moment to moment. Peter and Paul are each unique, particular instantiations of the human nature or essence. This means that each of them possesses all of the traits that are necessary and sufficient for membership in the class we call "human."[37] For Berkeleyan conceptualists, human nature is a universal, which is to say, an eternal archetype in the mind of God, reflecting key aspects of the divine nature (hence the term *imago Dei*) which is exemplified in various ways in particular human beings around the world and throughout history.

As for the complete idealist account of particulars, we must distinguish between inanimate and animate particulars. A particular *inanimate object*, such as an apple, is a mind-dependent collection or bundle of ideas or qualities (e.g., redness, smoothness, roundness, sweetness, crunchiness, etc.). But a particular *human being* is a combination of two things—an active, intelligent, substantial soul and a particular body (understood, again, as a bundle of unthinking, passive ideas or qualities). So Berkeleyan idealists affirm a kind of mind-body dualism, though they reject substance dualism. There is only one kind of substance, and that is mind/spirit. And there are two sub-categories of spirit—the one almighty divine Spirit (God) and finite, created spirits, which include human beings like Peter and Paul.

Finally, to say that Peter and Paul are resurrected from the dead is to say that after their earthly bodies perish, their spirits—which continue to exist despite the decay of their earthly bodies—are eventually conjoined with another human body (i.e., bundle of sensible properties) much like that which it possessed during this earthly existence. But their resurrection bodies will lack the degenerative tendencies that characterize living bodies

---

37. Exactly what are the necessary and sufficient characteristics for participating in the human essence is a matter of debate and beyond the scope of this chapter. Berkeleyan idealists would include in the list of essential human traits the possession of a certain kind of body and a certain kind of soul (perhaps inclusive of ultimate capacities for thinking, willing, and feeling), but presumably many specific models of human nature would be compatible with Berkeleyan idealism.

in this fallen world. This means their various bodily properties will enjoy a constancy throughout eternity which they do not display here.

3.2 PLATONISM RESPONSE—PAUL M. GOULD

Introduction

According to James Spiegel, idealism is the thesis that only minds and ideas exist. As George Berkeley famously stated, *to be is to be perceived or to be a perceiver*. Regarding the physical world, we are told that it "just is God's public ideas" (p. 84). Spiegel defends Berkeleyan idealism, the view that God, the divine mind, creates finite minds and mind-dependent physical reality, now understood as a collection of divine ideas.

The Physical World

Consider this apple. It's a concrete material object that has certain characteristics or qualities such as redness, roundness, and sweetness. Spiegel notes the charactered nature of concrete material objects and states without argument or fanfare, "What are these qualities but *ideas*" (p. 74). This is a mistake. Ideas or concepts mediate between the mind and the physical world, they do not constitute the physical world. Ideas are essentially intentional objects; properties, as Plato taught us, are intentionally inert.

Spiegel argues that there are no positive reasons for affirming the existence of mind-independent material objects. I find this claim striking. For it certainly *seems* as if there is a mind-independent physical world, and I take this as a good (positive) reason for thinking there *is* a mind-independent physical world. Of course, this *seeming* could be defeated if there are overriding reasons for doing so. What might those overriding reasons be? Spiegel offers four.

First, he argues that the notion of matter is unintelligible: "no one has ever perceived [a] material substratum," nor "can we even conceive it in our minds" (p. 73). Suppose substratum theory is unintelligible (a thesis I deny). So what? There are other accounts of material objects on offer, including the venerable Aristotelian account of substance offered in my lead essay, an account of particulars that Spiegel endorses in the case of living things.

Second, there is the argument from perceptual relativity. The fact that qualities of objects can be perceived differently depending on context and circumstance "strongly suggests mind-dependence of physical objects" (p. 74). How so, exactly? The idea seems to be that an object of direct awareness must have the properties or qualities that it appears to have. But, for example, a distant house can't be both small (as it appears from a distance) and large (as it appears up close). The fact of perceptual relativity is supposed to strongly suggest that the object of direct awareness in perceptual experience must be mind-dependent, removing the need to distinguish appearance from reality. I do not think the phenomena of perceptual relativity—or the cases of illusion or hallucination—provide overriding reasons for rejecting belief in an external physical world. Following Michael Huemer, we could argue that our house, understood as a mind-independent physical object, does change by talking on certain relational properties such as *being a certain angular size relative to distance x* and *being a certain angular size relative to distance y*, and so on, relative to a perceiver and the house.[38] Alternatively, the direct realist could reject the assumption that the object of our perceptual awareness must have the properties it appears to have. By distinguishing between the *object* of awareness (i.e., the mind-independent physical object) and the *vehicle* of awareness (i.e., the perceptual experience), and adopting, e.g., the adverbial theory of perception, the distinction between appearance and reality is rendered unproblematic.[39] Either way, the phenomena of perceptual relativity and the like do not give us reason to deny the belief in a mind-independent external world.

Third, there is an argument from quantum mechanics. On the Copenhagen interpretation of quantum mechanics, the properties of quantum systems are observer-dependent and this is supposed to support the belief that the physical world is mind-dependent. I'm happy to affirm the *consistency* of idealism with one possible interpretation of quantum mechanics. However, it does not follow that we find in this an "argument from science" (p. 74) for the *rational preferability* of Berkeleyian idealism or the Copenhagen interpretation of quantum phenomena.[40]

Finally, Spiegel claims that a "fairly straightforward" biblical argument for idealism can be made. Scripture teaches that God is the creator and sustainer of all distinct reality. Moreover, Scripture teaches that God is a mind or spirit and humans, created in God's image, are minds or spirits too. All

---

38. Huemer, *Skepticism and the Veil of Perception*, 120–24.

39. Huemer argues that the fundamental confusion of the indirect realist is a failure to properly distinguish between the *object* of awareness *of which* one is aware and the *vehicle* of awareness *by which* one is aware, Huemer, *Skepticism and the Veil of Perception*, 81.

40. For an account of an objective collapse interpretation of quantum mechanics that is fully realist about the microscopic and macroscopic realm, see Koons, "Knowing Nature: Aristotle, God, and the Quantum," 232–34. For an argument that quantum phenomena is suggestive of a neo-Aristotelian account of concrete material reality (an account I endorse), see Feser, *Aristotle's Revenge*, 310–30.

well and good. But then, according to Spiegel, from these facts "we can only conclude that the physical world is mind-dependent" (p. 75). I'll admit, I'm perplexed. I don't see even remotely, let alone straightforwardly, how those facts are supposed to entail the idealist thesis. Could we not believe, as the plain reading of Scripture seems to teach, that God created a distinct world, full of material and immaterial creatures and sustains them all in existence? On theistic idealism, God creates distinct-from-God finite spirits and sustains them. Why could he not do the same for a distinct-from-God physical world? Other problems are lurking. Spiegel seems to endorse creation *ex nihilo*. But if the physical world is just the maximal set of God's (sensory) ideas, then creation is not *ex nihilo*, it is *ex dei*. Worse, it seems that theistic idealism collapses into panentheism for now the physical world is quite literally part of God. This seems to me to be an objectionable sense of being "in" God that my participatory account of Christian Platonism ably avoids. There are no good reasons presented thus far for thinking that the physical world is mind-dependent.

Universals

I'm happy to read that Spiegel affirms universals as the best explanation for qualitative and resemblance facts. As to the ontological status of universals, he denies that they exist in some kind of Platonic heaven. Universals are divine ideas. I think this is the right way to go given his Berkeleyan idealism. But there are costs in taking this route that render theistic idealism unattractive. First, as already noted, ideas are not essentially intentional since they now are said to play a structure-making role when it comes to the physical world. This leads to an unlovely disjunctive account of ideas/concepts as either intentional objects or structure-making objects. Second, either the theistic idealist adopts a unified theory of predication and allows that God not only has ideas but exemplifies them too or a non-unified theory of predication and hold that God doesn't have properties/qualities and thus divine predicates don't refer to qualities/properties/ideas but something else. On the first option, God is a substance that *has* properties. But properties are just divine ideas. I suppose we should say here then that God has divine ideas in two ways: the divine idea *being all-powerful* stands in the parthood or constituency relationship with the divine mind and the exemplification relationship with the divine Substance. This picture—or something like it—is unlikely. On the second option, God is a simple substance; it is only finite substances that *have* properties. But if God is simple, then how can we meaningfully speak of God as having ideas? On the doctrine of divine simplicity, God has no metaphysical parts, aspects, or constituents. But then, it's not clear that theistic idealism is a coherent option. At the very least, we are owed an account of divine *and* human predication.

Particulars

Spiegel thinks there are only two kinds of particulars: immaterial substances and bundles of qualities. Living things are substances and substances are immaterial minds. Inanimate physical things—"footballs, cars, and apples" (p. 78)—are bundles of qualities. There are at least two problems with this picture. First, Spiegel doesn't seem to leave any room for plants. Plants are living things. But, according to Spiegel, living things possess minds. "A mind is an active perceiving conscious substance, essentially a thinking thing" (p. 80). Something must give: either plants are minds, i.e., active perceiving conscious thinking things, or the relevant demarcation between substances and non-substances is not the animate/inanimate divide. Second, some inanimate objects—e.g., carbon atoms, water molecules, and the like—possess a natural unity that suggests they are best categorized as substances. On the bundle theory, the parts of a thing are logically prior to the whole. In other words, the identity and existence of the whole is dependent on its parts. Thus, the bundle theory is most plausible when it comes to aggregates, including ordered aggregates, such as footballs and cars. But when it comes to apples—at least when they are part of a living tree—and carbon atoms, it seems that there is a kind of built-in teleology, along with irreducible properties and causal powers, suggestive of a substantial nature. Again, it seems a choice must be made: either deny the empirically plausible claim that atoms and apples possess a natural unity different in quality from footballs and cars or provide an account of the difference. That account of the difference between the natural and artificial unity of various inanimate physical objects, arguably, can't be given in terms of bundle theory alone.

Regarding the human soul, Spiegel argues that humans are souls that have bodies and bodies are just collections of (divine) ideas. This picture is a kind of dualism that is said to be superior to substance dualism since the interaction problem dissolves. There are two problems with this move. First, it seems that something like the interaction problem re-surfaces on the idealist picture, for now an account is needed of how immaterial (finite) substances interact with the collection of (divine) ideas that constitutes their body. This interaction problem seems worse than the original, for now I'm supposed to possess causal powers, at least if concurrentism is the way to go, over that cluster of divine ideas that constitute my body, so I'm supposed to have causal powers over some aspect or constituency of the divine mind. This seems like a problematic kind of power to possess over deity. Second, the idealist claim that my body is "a bundle of unthinking, passive ideas or qualities (p. 86) is difficult to square with the commonsense seeming that my body, and not just me, has causal powers of its own. Consider a traumatic brain injury. An injured brain will often lead to permanent mental dysfunction. This is evidence suggestive of two-way causal interaction between my body and my soul/mind. Moreover, if our earthly bodies decay, as Spiegel allows, it would seem, again, that our bodies do possess causal powers of their own. (For how could a body lose function and power unless it had function and power in the first place?) But bodies are passive and inert on theistic idealism, and thus bereft of any powers of their own.

Conclusion

As Peter van Inwagen reminds us, as fallible knowers, the "best we can do is believe what seems to us to be true unless we have some good reason to reject it."[41] But "idealism does not seem to us to be true," and "in fact, idealism seems to us to be false."[42] I agree with van Inwagen. We have no good reason to reject the belief that there exist objects external to minds.

3.3 ARISTOTELIANISM RESPONSE—TIMOTHY L. JACOBS

Introduction

James Spiegel models how a nuanced Christian metaphysic aims at biblical faithfulness while navigating intramural debates within idealism. At each fork the Bible guides his perspective. Our goals are similar: provide a faithful, rational Christian philosophy.

Method and Parsimony

Idealism follows Platonic and Cartesian mind-first, top-down, inside-out metaphysics, propagating the modern problem of proving other minds or the material world. Spiegel says this is "a problem that arguably is still unsolved" (p. 81). Just because idealists have not solved it, does not mean no

---

41. van Inwagen, *Metaphysics*, 67.
42. van Inwagen, *Metaphysics*, 67.

made Christianity seem less epistemically satisfying.[6] In the wake of this growing unrest, René Descartes sought to supply a new foundation upon which all knowledge could be built: "And thus I realized that once in my life I had need to raze everything to the ground and begin again from the original foundations, if I wanted to establish anything firm and lasting in the sciences."[7] In a thought experiment, Descartes decided to doubt everything that could be doubted, seeking something that could be known with absolute certainty. Once he found that which was indubitable, he believed he could reconstruct the totality of knowledge. This experiment was the paradigm shift in philosophy that moved us from the classical, to the modern epoch. In that shift, Descartes took metaphysics, and made it contingent on a new central disciple, namely epistemology.

Modern philosophy is an epoch that hinges on the quest for certitude. While classical philosophy would assert that we cannot know something is true unless we can know the reality to which that truth is connected, in modern philosophy we cannot know something is real, unless we can be certain of our ability to know true things. Descartes' doubt eventually brought him to his famous *cogito*, and the conclusion that he cannot truthfully doubt his own existence. From there, he used an ontological argument to prove God's existence, and therein bring back the exterior world and all that had been doubted. In making this move, Descartes believed he had given a new foundation for knowledge and established a way for those from around the various families of Christendom to have a common manner of reasoning.

As is often the case in philosophy, Descartes' well-intentioned endeavor had the opposite of his desired effect. The paradigmatic shift to an epistemology-based philosophic epoch was embraced by all but one of his contemporaries (Blaise Pascal), and was dominant for over two hundred years. Indeed, the story of modern philosophy is one of thinker after thinker presuming the Cartesian epistemology-centric approach to philosophy, but attempting different ways of embracing the exterior world. These attempts became increasingly more complex, more esoteric, eventually culminating in the works of Immanuel Kant and Georg Hegel. As sophisticated and expansive as these overarching systems of thought became, they never supplied a way by which to have direct access to, or certainty about, the world. Heidegger goes so far as to suggest that the goal of modern philosophy, particularly metaphysics, was the delusion that philosophy need to raise itself to the level of absolute science, as opposed to being that which undergirds

---

6. Balthasar, *Love Alone Is Credible*.
7. Descartes, *Discourse On Method*; and, *Meditations On First Philosophy*, 59.

science.[8] This quest for certitude, and the over-scientific, over-mechanistic approach to attempting to gain access to, and understanding of, the exterior world eventually led to its rejection, and the passing, in part, of the modern epoch.

By the late nineteenth century, thinkers like Kierkegaard and Nietzsche saw the work being done by modern philosophers as misguided. While they attempted to regain access to the exterior world, the entire question of meaning was all but absent. Here is when the shift to the third epoch begins. In classicalism, metaphysics was seen as the central discipline of philosophy, with the others contingent upon it, and in modernism, epistemology filled that role. The shift in these early existentialists and what will become the postmodern epoch sees questions of meaning and value, particularly questions related to ethics and aesthetics, as the center. This epoch places the question of *value* at the core, and sees questions of being and knowledge as dependent upon the categories of goodness and sensation.

Aspects of Postmodernism

I've belabored this brief history, to try and put postmodernism into a context befitting its name. The first use of the term "postmodern" was in 1929 by the Catholic theologian Bernard Iddings Bell in his work *Postmodernism and Other Essays*. Bell's concern with modernity was that, be it manifest in totalitarianism or liberalism, mankind had developed too strong a faith in reason. In fact, he thought that the two poles of liberalism and totalitarianism led to societies that were either culturally mediocre, or relied so heavily on scientific objectivity that people became spiritually weak and divested of metaphysical wonder.[9]

Drolet notes that Bell's use of the term "postmodern" "was rooted in an ancient skepticism about humans' ability to fathom the working of the universe and somehow change their place within it. The term's meaning was theological and conservative. Postmodernism stressed the mysterious and unknowable nature of the universe."[10] Obviously postmodernism took a drastic turn in the decades between Bell and Lyotard; however, the fundamental notion that the universe is mysterious and in many ways unknowable remained. Postmodernism is best seen as a direct reaction to, and rejection of, modernity. While modernity attempted to find with complete

---

8. Heidegger, *The Fundamental Concepts of Metaphysics*, 2.
9. Drolet, *The Postmodernism Reader: Foundational*, 4–5.
10. Drolet, *The Postmodernism Reader: Foundational*, 5.

certitude the absolute understanding of the world, postmodernity embraces the individual's subjective relation to the world.

Often postmodernity is seen as a rejection of absolute truth, in reality though, postmodernism is not overtly concerned with absolute truth, or with objective reality. Truth and reality may be objective, they may not be, but the modern project of trying to establish complete objectivity failed, so the concern is about how humanity lives. Perhaps put more plainly, while the modern philosopher might spend a fair amount of time attempting to prove if a chair exists, the postmodernist is happy to join the classicalist in simply sitting on the chair. That is not to say that the classicalist and the postmodernist agree on everything, by no means, but both reject the modernist obsession with, and criteria for, certitude, and that makes postmodernity in many ways a swing back toward the classical.

Postmodernism as an Ally to Christian Thought

Here we see the point in which Christianity and postmodernity ought not be seen at odds. Like most world religions, Christianity was birthed in the classical period, and therefore Christian theology presumes the existence of the exterior world, the primacy of metaphysical questions, the contingency of epistemology, ethics, and aesthetics, and any other features of classical thought. Obviously not everyone was a Christian in classical times, and so the apologetic endeavor was present, was mandated, and performed, but it was done presuming the classical philosophic ethos. The arguments for God's existence were not necessarily seen as means of converting the lost, but as a means of strengthening the faith of those who already believed. The desert fathers and mothers, Augustinian thought, medieval mysticism, and Thomism all placed a person's unbelief in either a darkened mind, or a darkened will, and in some cases both. Human rebellion, or frailty, was a limiter to human understanding. In all cases, the world was accessible, but humanity required illumination, or needed to be heightened in some manner, to fully understand the divine, and the cosmos.

As noted earlier, the Reformation and the birth of modern philosophy occurred within about a hundred years of each other. As both grew, they developed together. In part, what this union entailed was a mode of philosophical engagement that presumed the Cartesian system. This system reversed the classical mode in which God was presumed and humanity was understood in light of God, and instead placed the existence of humanity at the center, and the existence of everything else, including God, dependent upon humankind's ability to reason. In many ways, modernity itself is an inherently secular mode of philosophy, and its approach is overtly secularizing.

In order to engage with the increasingly blatant secular world, the church, the Protestant church in particular, began to embrace this modern secularized philosophical method, and placed on Christian theology and Christian Scripture expectations and tasks that were not their concern. In attempts to argue against the secularizing world, the church allowed its thought life and vernacular to change. A prime example is the manner in which the church allowed David Hume to change the definition of miracle, and instead of correcting him, played his game and allowed him to set the tone of the discussion for at least two centuries.[11]

Ultimately, what began to occur was that Christianity, a classical religion, was presented so fully within a secular modernist manner that Christianity began to secularize itself, with depth and meaning pulled away and the church turning into "resource" in the Heideggerian use of the term. Content stripped of meaning, and merely being available as a pliable tool.[12] This mode of thinking gave rise to the seeker-sensitive/church-growth or corporate-church model of Christianity, which sanitized, and in further ways secularized, Christianity.[13] Jesus as consumable commodity rather than Christ as it were. It was this approach to Christianity that the postmodern Christian influx was pushing against. Dan Kimball's *The Emerging Church*, and Robert Webber's Ancient-Future series (see, e.g., Webber, *Ancient-Future Worship*) in particular were rejections of a secularized, modernized Christianity, and initial thoughts toward postmodernity's ability to return to a more classical way of thinking.

Of course, this point is where the controversy arose. If Christianity is a classical faith, and modernity is a secular mode of thinking, but a secular mode of thinking that the church had embraced, then any correction that the postmodernist would make against the modernist church would feel

---

11. I've discussed this more fully in Welbaum "Defining Miracle: Hume, Theism and the History of a Concept."

12. For Heidegger, metaphysics is rooted in care, or meaning. The issue with modern technology is that it removes all contours. Journeys that should take months now take hours. People have the ability to talk to others anywhere in the world. The ideas of nearness and farness are flattened. Consider that Chicago-style pizza is a hallmark of the Windy City, but for a fee, I can have an authentic deep-dish pizza sent to me in California, and thanks to mass transit, someone in Chicago can have avocado toast in December. All geographic and temporal distinctions are eradicated and things lack meaning, and they do not condition individuals in the same manner. I will discuss this more in a later footnote. To see Heidegger's comments on technology, see Heidegger, *The Question Concerning Technology*, 127.

13. For a full discussion on this matter, see Guinness, *Dining with the Devil*.

like an attack on Christianity itself, as opposed the modernism it had embraced. Add to that the fact that postmodernity's focus on subjectivity can ignore objectivity altogether, meaning that the church was right to reject a good amount of what was being asserted, and you have the makings of a calamity of errors and misunderstanding.

I've spent a good amount of this chapter trying to present a picture in which the idea of "Christian postmodern metaphysics" makes sense as a category, even though postmodernity is often seen as anti-metaphysical, and anti-Christian. It is likely that I have both spent too much, and too little, time on this topic to make it completely helpful, but at this point hopefully we can conceive of postmodernism as a response to a secular, totalizing, modernistic metanarrative, which inhabited Christian thinking in a negative way. In the next few sections we will unpack further the harm of the modernistic metaphysic, and the manner of the postmodern response.

OBJECTIVITY AND SUBJECTIVITY AS FRIENDS, NOT FOES

Before going further, I need to address more fully the concern that many have about postmodernity's supposed rejection of objective, or absolute truth, and its embrace of subjectivity. Lyotard's statement that postmodernity is incredulity toward metanarratives seems disheartening when you are a part of a tradition that relies upon metanarratives. The discipline of metaphysics, and the entirety of the Christian faith, rests on the fact that things are a certain way. A thing is a thing, and the essence of that thing in some way exists and true things can be said of it. If such were not the case, then it would seem that everything is left to the individual's private interpretations, and indeed, in the postmodern epoch, that private interpretation, or communal interpretation, is brought to the center, as a reaction against the attempted scientific neutrality of modernity. The key concept here is that the idea of neutrality is a fiction. Let's consider assertions by two thinkers as a means of unpacking what is going on here.

First, in his *Fundamental Concepts of Metaphysics*, Martian Heidegger addresses possibly the most popular objection to postmodernity (broadly construed): "There are no absolutes? Are you absolutely sure about that?" In responding to this argument, Heidegger first notes that the ease at which the argument is asserted shows its weakness. The argument is concerned not with philosophy, or the content of an assertion, but with form.[14] Though he does not say it here, Heidegger is gesturing toward a Wittgensteinian notion

---

14. Heidegger, *Metaphysics*, 18.

related to the limits of language. Words do not relate to the world, words relate to other words and are used as gestures toward the world. Words do not describe the world in full, and not all language users use all words the same, so words are used in various language games as a means of gesturing to those who we believe use words the same way that we do. To make an assertion such as "There are no absolutes" may be contradictory in that it is an absolute statement, but Heidegger and Wittgenstein are talking about the world, not the language we use to describe or construct it. The proposition "There are no absolutes" being an absolute might create a paradox in language, but the proposition is language and therefor is a tool for describing the world, not necessarily a part of what is being described. It is a claim more about language than about reality. This objection then is more distraction than refutation.

This response will probably only be tenable to those who already hold that language is such that it does not describe the world but merely gestures to it. Heidegger's second response to the objection is perhaps more universally satisfying, "We are not in fact claiming, and never will claim, that it is absolutely certain that philosophy is not a science [absolutely certain knowledge]."[15] Heidegger's response to the question of absolutes is to say that he is not certain that there are no absolutes or that philosophy cannot find absolutes, merely that, as he sees it currently, that is not the case. In fact, the quest to have philosophy be a science, the quest to have philosophy find metaphysical and epistemological absolutes, is the quest to have philosophy—and by philosophy Heidegger means metaphysics—not be what philosophy actually is: a homesickness. Metaphysics is not concerned with the world *as it is*, it is concerned with the world *as it is constructed*. There may or may not be an objective way that things are, but my subjective construction is what matters.[16]

The second thinker I want to look to on this matter is Søren Kierkegaard. In his *Concluding Unscientific Postscript*, Kierkegaard writes, "Truth is subjectivity."[17] Some have pointed to this quote to show that Kierkegaard is a relativist, understanding his words to mean something akin to what Oprah or some other twenty-first-century celebrity means when they say, "Live your truth," but this is not Kierkegaard's aim. The motivation of the entirety of Kierkegaard's authorship is to understand how to be a Christian in Christendom, and as such to push against the dead faith of his contemporaries.[18]

---

15. Heidegger, *Metaphysics*, 18.
16. Heidegger, *Metaphysics* 18.
17. Kierkegaard, *Concluding Unscientific Postscript to Philosophical Fragments*, 185.
18. Kierkegaard, *The Point of View*, 90.

Kierkegaard refused to go to seminary to obtain theological training, because the seminaries were overrun with theology full of the mechanistic and scientific Kantian and Hegalian philosophy of late modernity, and the people he would end up preaching to might understand what he said intellectually, but would not believe it by faith. God would be like a scientific postulate to them, not a reality.

Here then we see the motivation behind Kierkegaard's desire to find a "truth that is true for him," to find a truth that is subjectively true. Modern philosophy cared little about what a person believed, and more what a person might intellectually "know" in an academic sense. Perhaps one of the more entertaining example of this can be found in Thomas Reid's chiding David Hume's denial of the certainty of the exterior world by noting that even Hume believes that he will have a readership, or that Hume's philosophy only makes sense in isolation.[19] If one does not know that there is a world, why does that world seem to be so real? Kierkegaard then said the academic is not what matters; it's the will, it's belief. We must find a truth that is true for us, in that it dictates our lives. This is subjective truth, truth that is known from the perspective of the one holding to it.

If left here, this would still seem to place Kierkegaard in the realm of relativism; however, there is only one truth that is objectively true, and therefore worthy of being our subjective truth, namely, the person of Jesus Christ. As Kierkegaard understands it, humans are made to be the single individual, the one leaving the heard and standing in right relationship with God. At that point a person is most herself, yet this happens only by leaping to faith in God, by means of her subjectivity. In the Kierkegaardian authorship, what we see is a person's existential evolution, as they progress from satisfying self, to finding a truth by which they might live, to eventually having that truth be in line with the creator of the universe.

Here we finally see the point to which this chapter's discussion has thus far been building, and the place at which we can begin to answer the question as to what a Christian postmodern metaphysic might look like. In some of his notebooks, Nietzsche asserted that there are no facts, only interpretations,[20] and building off that, Derrida said there is no outside-text, meaning everything must be read and interpreted within an immediate context.[21] Modernity attempted to find a place of neutral certitude, and in doing so created a mechanistic secular world. As a response to modernity's

---

19. Reid "Introduction" in *An Inquiry into the Human Mind, on the Principles of Common Sense*, 13–27.

20. Nietzsche and Kaufmann, *The Portable Nietzsche*, 458.

21. Derrida, *Of Grammatology*, 158.

inability to find objectivity, postmodernity embraced subjectivity, and the experience of the individual.

However, the Christian postmodernist, the thinker in the vein of Kierkegaard, Pascal, and perhaps even Augustine, sees that the subjective and the objective are not contradictory unless they contradict. James K. A. Smith notes, "Even the right interpretation is an interpretation."[22] The Christian postmodernist acknowledges her human frailty, her inability to know things beyond her scope, and the inherent subjectivity of her knowledge and of her world, but that does not mean that there is not an objective way that things actually are, toward which our subjectivity ought to point. For this reason, a Christian postmodern metaphysic is one that actually does not necessarily contradict other views (though it may), because while they are aiming at understanding the objective world as it is, the postmodernist is concerned with the subjective world as it is constructed. In fact, the key postmodern thinkers: Lyotard, Foucault, Deleuze, and Derrida are in reality all asking the same question, namely, "How is our subjective world of meaning constructed?" They each approach it from different field, or different avenue, narrative, power/knowledge, difference, and language respectively, but ultimately it is a question of constructive subjectivity.

It is for this reason, in part, that I've chosen to define the term, and the epoch, of postmodernity so broadly. The thinkers most often called postmodernists are insightful and helpful in the area of human subjectivity, but much of their work is pulling from the existential, phenomenological, linguistic, and continental thinkers that comprised the greater part of the twentieth century. Truthfully, the are all merely applications of Nietzsche, Wittgenstein, and Heidegger, with the latter being the greatest influence. Further, while the study of human subjectivity is vitally important, the harmful wing of the emerging church movement only focused on subjectivity, as opposed to seeing subjectivity as *our experience* of *objective reality*. The Christian thinker must embrace both.

The Ontic and the Ontological

Perhaps the most profound legacy of Descartes' philosophy was the fragilization of the epistemic certainty of the exterior world. Much of the work of modern philosophy was an attempt to gain certainty that the exterior world exists, or answer the question of how we can speak confidently about the exterior world without having to rely on an ontological argument for God's existence, or in many cases, on the existence of a God at all. The

22. Smith, *Who's Afraid of Postmodernism?* 45.

intensity of the question increased in the work of David Hume. Hume, an empiricist, came to very few, if any, positive conclusions about humanity's ability to have knowledge, but was very skeptical about our ability to know much of anything. For Hume everything that a person knows comes via sense data, but that data is merely associated with other sense data by the mental faculty of imagination. There is no way to know substance, identity, or cause and effect in the real world. The world remained unknowable. This fact is why Hume said that abstruse thought leads to melancholy and endless uncertainty.[23]

Upon reading Hume's work, Immanuel Kant says he was awoken from his dogmatic slumber, and he then attempted to provide a way in which Hume's thought could still give some connection to the exterior world.[24] Kant's system involved creating a distinction between the world in and of itself, and the world as it appears to a person. The world in and of itself was almost entirely unreachable. Instead, this world could only be known as sense experience, and that sense data was processed through a priori structures of the mind, what Kant called the categories, by the faculty of imagination, in order to create a phenomenon, or an appearance. Kant's move here was an attempt to affirm Hume's theses, and simultaneous reject his conclusions by restoring direct access to an, if not the, exterior world. However, what Kant actually did was create a means of metaphysical speculation in which the world in and of itself (Kant calls this the noumenal world) is unknowable, and the world as it appears to me (the phenomenal world) is what actually matters.[25]

This history is of note to us because Heidegger picks up on this distinction. However, instead of the noumenal and the phenomenal, Heidegger speaks about the ontic, and the ontological. He notes that much metaphysical error has come from the confusion of these two categories. The ontic is the world of matter, the world of stuff. The ontological is the world of being. So often metaphysics will attempt to define the ontic world by means of the ontological, or will presume that the ontological world in some way transfers to the ontic, but it does not. While in Kant's system, the mind takes sense data from the noumenal world to construct the phenomenal world

---

23. Hume, *An Enquiry Concerning Human Understanding*, 5–6.

24. While a topic for another time, I would like to note that I believe a case can be made that there is very little original in Kantian metaphysics, and that it is better to see Kantian metaphysics as Humean metaphysics with greater explanation.

25. I have painted with a broad brush here, but my approach to philosophy is always seated in history, but for the sake of space I have need to speed history up a few clips and truncate some matters.

that one interacts with, in Heidegger's system, Dasein (the human) projects itself onto the ontic world and creates the ontological.[26]

An example may be helpful. Heidegger at one point speaks of the relationship between a bench and a house.[27] In the ontic world there is no such thing as a bench, nor is there a house. There is just matter. Perhaps we can push it a bit and say there is just wood. What there is plenty of, however, is potential. This matter has the potential to be a certain thing, that matter has the potential to be that certain thing, etc. The ontic world is one of material extension and material differentiation. The material in the ontic world has properties, and uses, but it lacks meaning. In the ontological world however, meaning abounds.

It has been a long time coming, but here we finally begin to see the answers to some of the questions at the heart of this book. For Heidegger, and the postmodern thinkers who follow him, mankind's concern is not with the *essence* of a thing, but the *meaning* of a thing. There is no bench, there is no house, there is this bench, and there is this house. What we call a bench, or a house, is collection of wooden material that a craftsman built, for an intended purpose, a purpose that Dasein cares about because he has sore legs, or the need for shelter. Out of this care, Dasein projects meaning upon the possibilities presented by this material, and in so doing creates the world in which he lives.[28] This is a world that includes benches and houses as meaningful concepts, but not because these items exist in a meaningful way in the ontic world, but rather because they exist within the individual's care structure, and in that way are a part of the worlding of the world.

The term "worlding" may sound a bit odd, and rest assured, it is. The later Heidegger has a similar idea that he calls "thinging." Roughly what Heidegger is doing by adding "ing" to the end of these words is drawing attention to the process whereby they become what they are. Think of it this

26. Heidegger, particularly in his earlier work, prefers not to use the terms "mankind" or "person," seeing them as laden with preconditions to thought that already presume a type of thinking. He understands "mankind" to be rooted in Greek thought, and "personhood" to be rooted in Christianity. He discusses this fully in Heidegger, *Ontology*. Instead, Heidegger uses the German word "sein," which means "being" combined with the prefix "Da," meaning either "here" or "there." His focus is that we are beings, but our focus cannot be on what it means to be a being, rather what is being. As beings, we are beings for whom being is an issue. We are the only entities that create meaning, give identity, and are aware of our state of existence. The use of "Dasein" is a move by Heidegger to wipe away everything that came before, and to understand humans as primarily existences among other existences, since his fundamental approach to ontology is one of dynamic interrelation as opposed to austere separation.

27. Heidegger, *The Metaphysical Foundations of Logic*, 127.

28. Note, the later Heidegger would rail against technology's penchant for stripping away meaning, and leaving something as merely a resource.

way, what makes a dog a dog? Plato would say "dogness," focusing on the unique, set apart, unchangeable essence that makes a dog a dog. Heidegger would say that a dog is a dog by the way that the dog dogs, or another way, a dog is a dog by the doging of the dog. There is a manner in which a dog exists. A way in which it acts, in which is relates to other objects, and most importantly, a way in which it discloses itself to Dasein. People say they are "dog people" or that they like their cat because it acts like a dog, and in these situations people are looking at the relationships, the care, the concern, and the contentions that these animals have with others, and projecting meaning and being onto the dog. The entity, the animal, exists onticaly, man's best friend is projected ontologically.

We find ourselves in an ontic world. Heidegger rejects the modern idea of radical skepticism about the exterior world. The world exists. We can study it, we can learn things about it. However, the ontic world of brute fact becomes the ontological world of meaning through my worlding of the world. In the same way that your cubicle or your office at work initially starts off as a foreign space to you but eventually becomes home or your place of belonging, so does the world go from being space to place for Dasein. As we exist, we project ourselves onto the ontic world, and in so doing, create the world in which we exist. Since we are communal beings, that projection also includes projecting meaning on other Dasein, and their projecting meaning onto me, and our mutual projecting meaning onto the world. This mutual and social projection is how we create the world of collective meaning that we all share.

The postmodern concern is not with the ontic world, but with the ontological world. Kant and Hume are correct in the postmodern mind, any time that we approach the world, we do so in a manner mediated by our senses, but further than that, we do so in a way mediated by our situatedness. Unlike the modernist dream, a person is not distinct from nature, as the ancients and medieval were well aware, a person is a part of the created order, a part of a dynamic and vibrant cosmos. I do not approach the world as one who is outside it as a third party observer; rather, I am an active participant in the world, participating from my place of situatedness. I am thrown into a world that exists prior to me, full of concerns, meaning, and care that I am taught, that I learn, and that I embody, and then as I progress, I react to and challenge and grow within that world as the world forms me, and I respond to it by forming the world that I inhabit.

We are social creatures, so that world is shared, but the world that two people find meaningful will not necessarily be identical. Both worlds are based upon interpretation. According to Derrida, everything is a text; everything is interpretation. The world of meaning, what we consider the sphere of ontology, is an interpretation, or perhaps a projection, of the self in relation to the ontic world, in light of other persons, and our situatedness with one another within our spatio-temporal existence. A postmodern metaphysic is a study on the use of words, and the means of fostering and cultivating meaning, and care, as one interprets the world in which one lives. To this end we can see why so many within the secular postmodern sphere speak of coping with existence, since their manner of thought is aimed at making sense of life subjectively, untethered from the objective.

How then can a Christian postmodern metaphysic exist? Christians believe in truth, postmodernism rests on interpretation. God is objectively real, postmodernism is concerned with the subjectively real. Christianity rests in a classicalist mode of thinking rooted in metaphysics, postmodernity rests primarily on concerns of value or aesthetics/ethics. The path forward here is actually surprisingly simple. While it is true that the postmodern mind understand everything as interpretation, we return to James K. A. Smith's assertion, "Even the right interpretation is an interpretation."

A Christian Postmodern Metaphysical Framework

Metaphysics is the study of reality. It asks questions related to essence, nature, substance, identity, and so on. Postmodernism understands those questions to be ones of societal and individual construction. When I make a statement about the identity of an object, I am not stating a universal about the object in and of itself, but rather about how I understand the object, or perhaps how the object is revealing itself to me. Christianity understands that God created all things, sustains all things, and moves sovereignly over all things.

As I understand it then, the Christian postmodern metaphysician is the one who understands that God is the creator. As creator, God knows objectively what He made. God is omniscient, so He also knows every possible interpretation or approach to His created world that might exist. He also knows perfectly everything that will be invented, how it might be better, how it might be worse, the intent behind it, etc. God has complete knowledge, and that knowledge is as the creator, observer, sustainer, corrector, etc., of the universe and all that is within it. God has complete objective knowledge of all things. It could be asked about His subjective knowledge, but as we are discussing metaphysics, we see within the Divine the complete fusion of objective and subjective reality. To that extent, I don't believe that the Christian postmodern metaphysic is at odds with any of the other chapters in this book. The concern for the postmodernist is not the objectivity/subjectivity of the infinite, but of the finite.

Humans are finite creatures. Within our finitude there are limits to what can be known. In Eden, and in heaven, those limits will perhaps be different, but due to our creaturely nature, we still lacked/will still lack omniscience. In those situations the known is still known from my perspective, and if God's perspective is the correct perspective, the truly objective perspective, what I can know will be a fragment of that. Our aim is to have the mind of God, not in that we are omniscient, we can't even become "mostly-scient," rather that we agree with God.

This situation is exacerbated in our present state as we suffer the consequences of sin. Sin has darkened our reason, and placed it out of step with its proper function. In the wake of Descartes' *cogito*, Pascal said, "The heart has its reasons that reason knows not."[29] Pascal dismissed the Cartesian system as "useless and uncertain."[30] Reason is not the key to understanding the fallen world; it is imagination. In an unfallen state, Pascal asserts that reason would prove what is right, and imagination would make one desire what is right; however, in our postlapsarian state, reason is dominated by imagination, and at best works to support that which is imagined. Pascal notes that if you take the most reasonable man, a philosopher, and put him on a board over an infinite chasm, even if he knows the board is sturdy and will support his weight, he will soon be in a cold sweat.[31] Our subjective experience overpowers our rational faculties constantly. There can be no objectivity by those with wills and minds that have been tainted by sin. The heart rebels, and head will attempt to validate the actions of the heart. This is an application of the Augustinian/Anselmian belief that "faith seeks understanding," the mind does not intellectually form beliefs; the mind supports beliefs that form in us.

To that end, Christian postmodern metaphysics looks very much like presuppositional apologetics, or Reformed epistemology. Or Alistair McGrath's thesis in *The Open Secret*, where humans have a type of visual agnosia, unable to properly interpret what is in front of us, so we instead create other understandings of the world.[32] Due to our finitude, and our brokenness, mankind constructs subjective understandings of the world that are very real to us, but are out of step with objective reality. Secular postmodern philosophy stops at this point. Everything that we believe is

---

29. Pascal, *Pensées*, 216, S680/L423.
30. Pascal, *Pensées*, 133, S445/L887.
31. Pascal, *Pensées*, 13, S78/L44.
32. McGrath, *The Open Secret*.

a result of power games, stories we tell ourselves, or the way that language is used as means to quantify, or place grids on the ineffable. However, the ineffable is the ontic, the realm of objective reality, where the world is as it actually is in and of itself, as created by and sustained by God. Coming into contact with this is the feeling of the Kantian sublime, the feeling of being overwhelmed.[33] When one realizes that one's finitude leads to the creation of subjective realities that might actually fail in light of objective reality, this is where one begins to approach reality with the passion of infinity, and becomes the Knight of Faith, for Kierkegaard, the one who sees all creation as a gift and comes in right relationship with God, aligning his subjective to God's objectivity, and seeking then to interpret the world in light of objective reality.

All that said, Christian postmodernists can believe in objective essences and universals, but their focus is on the construction of the subjective worlds of meaning that we inhabit. We must find a truth that is true for us, in that, we must find that which we hold to passionately, with the full force of our soul. The only right object of our soul's passion is the source of objective reality, but the nature of that reality matters only so much when the hearts in rebellion do whatever can be done to flee and create alternate realities as a means of escaping the objective.

The subjective and situated nature of postmodernity makes the understanding of the soul necessarily either materialist or hylomorphic. In secular postmodernity, there is no spiritual soul; the idea of soul merely means life essence, or passion, what Heidegger would call being, and a being's care structure, which constructs a world of meaning. This world of meaning is dependent upon our relationships with the world and with others in the world. Our identity, our soul, is contingent on these connections. The Christian postmodernist would affirm the importance of relationships in identity, noting, however, that the relationship with the divine is the driving source of our actual identity. For the Christian, the soul is the self, humans are necessarily physical, so the Christian postmodernist would sit very close to the Thomistic understanding of the soul in which I am actually the union of my body and my soul, with the acknowledgement that the body changes overtime, and the soul does not.

Case Study

As we come to an end, we turn our attention to our dear Peter and Paul of whom you thus far have read three other accounts. Peter and Paul are made

33. Kant, *Critique of Judgment*, 246–59.

in God's image, they lived, they died, and they will be resurrected. How does a Christian postmodern metaphysic make sense of this reality?

First, we must realize that this is the teaching of Scripture, the means whereby God reveals Himself to us. The promise of the resurrection then is an objective truth that Christians hold to as their subjective truth, looking with joy and hope toward the promise of resurrection. In the resurrection, Peter and Paul will still be soul-body hybrids, in which their soul is united with a reconstituted physical body. There is no concern as to whether the particles that create the bodies of Peter and Paul are in fact the same particles that comprised their body on earth, because those particles were in constant flux. As you read this book your body's cellular and particle composition is changing. Your hair is growing, your skin is dying, you are gaining or losing weight. What matters is the identity that persists over time. That identity rests upon one's self-relationship, relationship to the world, and relationship to God. In the resurrection, the souls of Peter and Paul remain the same, the body is reconstituted, and the primary social connection that forms the bases of their identity, namely the relationship with God, remains the same.

When resurrected, Peter and Paul will exist, as they have since their creation. By exist I merely mean, "to be." They are Dasein, being-there, beings among other beings. On Earth they "being-ed" one way, in the intermediate state another, and in the resurrection yet another, but in all three they are beings in relation to other beings, and exist as held in existence by the grounding of all beings, the self-existent God.[34] They maintain being what they are, human, and they are both equally human, but the postmodern concern is less about how two humans can be particulars of the same essence, and more about what it means to live out their full humanity, or rather, to live in relation with other entities, and create subjective reality in line with objective reality. To that end, if to be human is to be made in God's image, and made to worship Him completely, the Christian postmodern concern about existence and universals is less about their nature, and more about the actions and relationships that are indicative of full humanity. Is there an essence to being human? Certainly, but its existence matters little if

---

34. Please note that here Heidegger would accuse me of doing "ontotheology" because I am synthesizing theology and metaphysics. This concept though comes from an understanding in which God must be left out of metaphysical speculation because it both cheapens the concept of God and eliminates the work of actual metaphysics. This concern is where the early Heidegger goes farther then merely rejecting modernity, but sees classical metaphysics, particularly Platonic metaphysics, as most erroneous too, given the inclusion of the divine. The later Heidegger makes use of the concept of "divinities" when understanding the metaphysical composition of all "things" but understands them as only one part of a fourfold structure, also including the earth, sky, and mortals. Their function is less to be gods, and more to be sources of awe and meaning.

it is not embodied properly, in Peter and Paul's subjectivity aligning with objective reality, and therein the performance of their full subjectively objective humanity. Also, Paul would probably still be a rather good tent builder, and Peter would remember losing a footrace to John.

4.2 PLATONISM RESPONSE—PAUL M. GOULD

Introduction

In his lead essay, Sam Welbaum sets out to justify the postmodern seat at the Christian metaphysical table and to show that a postmodern approach to metaphysics is "more of an ally to Christianity than previously thought" (p. 104). Unfortunately, I don't think the lead essay accomplished either of these stated goals. I'll organize my complaint around four themes.

A Potted History

Welbaum begins with a sweeping historical survey of the main trends in philosophical thought over the past 2,500 years, organized into the classical, modern, and postmodern eras. At the 14,000-foot level, the story Welbaum provides is familiar and in the main correct. But embedded within this admittedly brief account, there are claims that can and should be challenged, and in challenging these claims, his overall theses are rendered suspect. I have two worries.

First, Welbaum claims that for each era, one philosophical sub-discipline was viewed as fundamental whereas the rest were thought derivative. In the classical era, "metaphysics was seen as the central discipline of philosophy, with the others contingent upon it" (p. 107). Likewise, as the story continues, in the modern era, "epistemology filled that role" (p. 107). By the time we arrive at the postmodern era, "the question of value [is] at the core, and [the postmodern epoch] sees questions of being and knowledge as dependent upon the categories of goodness and sensation" (p. 107). This language of "contingent upon" or "dependent upon" is misleading. While it may be true that various philosophical issues and concerns were more prominent or pressing in one era over another, it does not follow that this renders one sub-discipline as fundamental and the others as derivative in any of these eras. Philosophy is not that cut and dry nor are the various sub-disciplines as hermetically sealed off from one another as Welbaum suggests. I'm not convinced that this narrative is *descriptively* accurate. But even if Welbaum's story is an apt description of the way things unfolded historically in philosophy, it doesn't follow that there is any *prescriptive* lesson we should learn from it. By my lights, metaphysical questions are fundamental, no matter what era we find ourselves in. In order to do epistemology or axiology well, we must first address the compulsory questions in metaphysics (more on that below).

Second, Welbaum gives too much credit to modern philosophy and too little credit to the church in explicating the secularizing forces at play during the modern period. In a desperate attempt to remain relevant we are told that "the church, the Protestant church in particular, began to embrace this modern secularized philosophical method, and placed on Christian theology, and Christian Scripture, expectations and tasks that were not its concern" (p. 108), that the church "*allowed* David Hume to change the definition of miracle" (p. 109 emphasis mine), and that this secular "mode of thinking gave rise to the seeker-sensitive/church-growth, or corporate-church, model of Christianity, which sanitized, and in further ways secularized Christianity" (p. 109). Quite a lot of causal power laid at the feet of modern philosophy! Quite a bit of agency removed from the church too! But this account is an oversimplification. As others have pointed out, the problems that led to disenchantment have their roots in pre-modernity (or what Welbaum would prefer to call the classical period). More specifically, there were moves made in theology during the late medieval age—well before the time of Descartes—that sowed the seeds of secularization that came to fruition in the modern period.[35] Yes, we should reject the myth of neutrality, the hope of epistemic certainty, and hubris of a kind of rigid rationalism. But these false ideas have their roots in the shift from realism, along with a belief in essences or natures, to nominalism and voluntarism, and these shifts took place in theology first, not philosophy. To miss these historically prominent changes in outlook is to truncate the story of the history of thought in the West. And it also will lead, as it does in Welbaum's case, to the idea that postmodernism is an improvement that corrects all the evil missteps made in modernity, and modernity alone.

A Confusion about Seeing

As far as I can tell, Welbaum endorses the idea that language doesn't describe the world, rather it "gestures to it" (p. 111). He seems to approve the idea, advanced by Heidegger, that "Metaphysics is not concerned with the world as it is, it is concerned with the world as constructed" (p. 111). And

---

35. For a nice summary of the details, see Boersma, *Heavenly Participation*, 52–83. See also Leff, *The Dissolution of the Medieval Outlook*.

following Kierkegaard, we are told that "We must find a truth that is true for us, in that it dictates our lives. This is subjective truth, truth that is known from the perspective of the one holding to it" (p. 112). To avoid the slide to relativism, Welbaum reminds us, again following Kierkegaard, that "there is only one truth that is objectively true, and therefore worthy of being our subjective truth, namely, the person of Jesus Christ" (P. 112). All of this is supposed to help us see "what a Christian postmodern metaphysic might look like" (p. 112). The idea is that a Christian postmodern metaphysics embraces subjectivity since everything is an interpretation anyhow.

All of this is confused, for at least two reasons. First, Welbaum leaves no room for "simply seeing." All reality is mediated-reality: we see the ball *as* a ball, and we see *that* the ball is red. But we can't just simply see the red ball, according to Welbaum, because then we'd be directly acquainted with reality, and that is not possible given our "situatedness." This is a mistake. We are not trapped behind our concepts and language. Rather, our concepts and language help us express or describe the world as it is (however imperfect it might be at times).[36] We can get things right, and we can know truths, beyond the "one objective truth" of Jesus Christ (I'm not entirely sure what that is supposed to mean). I can know, through direct acquaintance that there is a red ball before me. And I can know that "the ball is red" (i.e., I can have propositional knowledge). Thus, it is not the case that there is "one objective truth." That's just not how the correspondence theory of truth works. Rather, truth obtains when we stand in a right relationship to reality, or more accurately, when the propositional content of our beliefs or statements corresponds to facts about the world. Welbaum admits there is a mind-independent (i.e., an objective) world, created by God. Welbaum owes us an account of objective reality as well as an account of how the objective and subjective relate (I agree, but it is a trivial truth, that "The Christian thinker must embrace both" (p. 113).)

Second, Welbaum confuses metaphysical and epistemic notions of truth and objectivity. The moderns were not wrong about metaphysical truth. They believed truth is discoverable and can be known. Welbaum seems to equate the search for "objective truth" or "absolute truth" with the quest for certainty and the myth of neutrality. But this is a confusion. It is possible to believe truth is objective without thinking that we must know the truth with certainty or that we are neutral observers. These latter epistemic claims are not part of the notion of metaphysical truth, and Welbaum, with his appeals to "your subjective truth," seems to conflate them in his essay.

36. For a defense of these claims, see Moreland and DeWeese, "The Premature Report of Foundationalism's Demise," 81–107. See also Willard, "How Concepts Relate the Mind to Its Objects," 5–20.

Welbaum acknowledges the "harmful wing of the emerging church movement [that] only focused on subjectivity" but his essay does little to help the reader understand his view of metaphysical truth and its connection to (the distinct) first-person subjective perspective. I suspect this omission is due to the confusion noted here. Minimally, I would invite further clarification.

A Failure to Answer Compulsory Questions

Metaphysics studies the nature and structure of reality. At times, Welbaum acknowledges this traditional understanding of metaphysics. As such, metaphysics seeks to answer key questions about the kinds of things that exist and their nature and relations. Thus, for any robust metaphysic, Christian or otherwise, there are certain compulsory questions that must be answered. A survey of any contemporary metaphysics textbook will give an idea of the kinds of questions to be explored and accounts of the world that are needed. In addition to the three tasks and methods I spelled out in my lead essay, a robust metaphysic will address the notion of substance, causation, time, space, property, relation, modality, identity, and more. Welbaum's essay failed to answer, as far as I can tell, any of the compulsory questions of metaphysics. Instead, we are given Heidegger's distinction between the ontic and the ontological. The ontic is "the world of matter, the world of stuff" and the ontological "is the world of being" (p. 114). I have no idea what this is supposed to mean in this context. What is matter? What is stuff? What is being? Welbaum gives little guidance. He does note that "The ontic world is one of material extension and material differentiation. The material in the ontic world has properties, and uses, but it lacks meaning" (p. 115). If I didn't know better, I'd say Welbaum's "ontic" world is populated by neo-Humean corpuscles, the very thing we were told, as a product of the modern era, ought to be anathematized! Perhaps the problem is we're not supposed to care about these compulsory questions. According to Welbaum, "the postmodern concern is not with the ontic world, but with the ontological world" (p. 116). This is because "mankind's concern is not with the essence of things, but the meaning of things" (p. 116). This is a false dichotomy at best, and at worst (and I suspect the worst) it renders a postmodern metaphysic impossible. Questions of meaning are inextricably tied to questions of metaphysics. And it is not obvious, in fact I think it false, to think that there is only a subjective meaning landscape. For on the Christian story, everything is endowed with meaning because of God. There is objective meaning in the world and that meaning exists even if there were no humans to appreciate or attend to it (this is secured on my account given the participatory nature of reality).

This is a book on Christian metaphysics. It ought to answer at least some of the compulsory questions that metaphysics seeks to investigate. Welbaum's essay leaves them unanswered.

The Demarcation Problem

Finally, there is the question of demarcation. What is distinctive, the *sine qua non*, of a Christian postmodern metaphysic? I'm not sure, after reading this essay. Welbaum doesn't believe that "the Christian postmodern metaphysic is at odds with any of the other chapters in this book" (p. 117), that it "looks very much like presuppositional apologetics, or Reformed epistemology" (p. 118), and that "the Christian postmodernist can believe in objective essences and universals, [even as] their focus is on the construction of the subjective world of meaning that we inhabit" (p. 119). With such a big tent, I'm left wondering what distinctive tenet or tenets demarcate the Christian Platonist, Aristotelian, and idealist from the postmodern?

The case study doesn't set the postmodern metaphysic apart from any of the other views, as far as I can tell, given the lack of detail provided beyond the basic deliverances of Scripture. The claim that "the subjective and situated nature of postmodernity makes the understanding of the soul necessary either materialist or hylomorphic" (p. 119) is opaque (at best) and false. If anything, our subjectivity is inconsistent with a materialist position and some version of dualism (Cartesian, Thomistic, emergent) is entailed by the reality of phenomenal consciousness. This unclarity, unfortunately, has been noted as a demarcating line between a more analytic, precision-oriented approach to philosophy and continental (or postmodern) philosophy. I invite Professor Welbaum, in his concluding reply, to relocate that familiar line.

4.3 ARISTOTELIANISM RESPONSE— TIMOTHY L. JACOBS

Introduction

I appreciated Sam Welbaum's approach and desire to stay faithful to orthodoxy. While I disagree with his metaphysics, he displays a genuine search for biblical truth. He provides some insight on how to be a Christian postmodern despite postmodernism's checkered past. However, I think much still remains unclear.

The Subjective Objectivism of Being-There in the Worlding World, or the Meaning of Meaning, or Something Like That

Welbaum says, "A postmodern metaphysic is a study on the use of words, and the means of fostering and cultivating meaning, and care, as one interprets the world in which one lives" (p. 116). For all its effort to study the meanings of words, it does more to obscure them. What is the meaning of *being-there, being-ed,* or *the worlding of the world*? Familiar words are used in new and confusing ways, like *ontic, ontological, matter, subjectivism, objectivism, essence, hylomorphism,* "your" *truth, interpretation, care structure, absolutes,* etc. Where these words are borrowed from other systems, the contexts that give them meaning are undermined. Nietzsche critiqued the Enlightenment for doing the same with ethics.

Meaning is a notoriously ambiguous term in postmodernism. It sounds profound and mysterious. Robert Nozsick says we hardly know what we mean when we ask "What is the meaning of life?"[37] Douglas Adams poked at this by answering "42." Nozsick says we could be referring to man's chief end, life after death, God's plan for our lives, our lasting effect on the world, universal teleology, or other meanings. The meaning of life is this: the chief end of man is to glorify God by enjoying him forever, constituted in the Christlike virtues of the fruit of the Spirit. We do not make a subjective interpretation of this, we live out this universal truth in our personal lives in a personal relationship with Christ. Is that all postmodernism means? In Aristotelian or Platonic metaphysics, *meaning* is first and foremost how a term refers to reality. Wittgenstein is right that meaning depends on contextual use, but his "language games" are often misunderstood as relativistic or postmodern. On the contrary, his prize followers, Anscombe, Geach, and Kenny, all took him as a realist critiquing Cartesian skepticism about the external world.

Truth is when a proposition corresponds to reality. Aristotle said, "To say of what is that it is not, or of what is not that it is, is false, while to say of what is that it is, and of what is not that it is not, is true."[38] Mind-independent reality and propositions that accurately represent it are real and true

---

37. Nozick, "Philosophy and the Meaning of Life," 571–610.
38. *Metaphysics* 1011b25.

for everyone. While Welbaum affirms objective, mind-independent reality, *meaning* and *truth* are framed subjectively. His use of "your truth," "real to us," "construction of the subjective worlds of meaning," and the like have no clear meaning. He says, "There is only one truth that is objectively true, and therefore worthy of being our subjective truth, namely, the person of Jesus Christ." I am not sure what *objective* and *subjective* mean in this context. Does he mean we should both know the truth and live it? Then say so with familiar language. Subjectivist language obscures the truth.

Metaphysics or Ethics?

When pressed, new words often turn out to have old meanings. Applying truth becomes "live *your* truth." Applying universal principles in your personal contexts and relationships becomes "being-there." Benevolence becomes "the individual's care structure" as people change the world, or "the worlding of the world." These are ethical concepts telling us to act in certain ways. Much of postmodern metaphysics turns out to be ethics wrapped in relativistic metaphysics. Meanwhile, it leaves metaphysical questions unanswered because it supposedly is not concerned with those questions. We have always known ethics and metaphysics are concerned with different questions because they are different sciences, but the topic at hand is metaphysics, not ethics.

Welbaum says, "Metaphysics is the study of reality. It asks questions related to essence, nature, substance, identity, and so on. Postmodernism understands those questions to be ones of societal and individual construction" (p. 117). Really? God's essence is a societal construct? Is Christ both God and man? What are we to make of human nature, fallen or not, and our identity as the image of God? Welbaum says Christ is the only objective truth and that the soul is probably hylomorphic. On what basis can Welbaum claim this? If metaphysics is not concerned with these questions, how can we defend against historic heresies? Welbaum says, "Metaphysics is not concerned with the world as it is, it is concerned with the world as it is constructed. There may or may not be an objective way that things are, but my subjective construction is what matters" (p. 111). But I want to know about the world *God* constructed, not my own fancy. I want to follow truths I discover, not interpretations I create. If I cannot have access to reality, I am truly trapped in my own ideas and can only degrade into modernist skepticism about everything. I have no means of establishing certainty about anything because I have no access to reality.

Realism

Much is made of truth being a construct or interpretation or relationship. The relationship between objectivism and subjectivism is as unclear as the terms used to explain them. It is claimed that postmodernism solves modernity's skepticism about the external world by admitting that we cannot have direct and reliable knowledge of reality. We are trapped by our worldview, unable to see the world as it is. Far from rejecting modernist problems, postmodernism compounds them, just as idealism does. All that can be said in this limited space is that if we were inescapably wrapped in our worldview with no ability to see things from a neutral perspective, I am not sure how we could know it. Uncertainty presupposes certainty, by definition, as the former is a privation of the latter. Certainty is needed for doubt to be possible.

We do in fact have direct sensory access to reality. It is true that our perceptions may be mistaken or our interpretations may be wrong, but these are cured with more observation, not a rejection of the reliability of observation. If I thought I saw someone I know, my mistake is cured with a double take, not "Well, I guess I can never trust my eyes again." My mistaken beliefs are cured by more evidence and reasoning. Welbaum denies the secular postmodern claim that "everything is left to the individual's private interpretations," but he does not justify his denial. It is true that "everything is an interpretation" insofar as an interpretation is just a judgment or representation of reality that can be perfectly accurate or not. That does not imply any subjectivism. I do not need "neutrality" or modernism's mythical objective "God's eye view" to know the truth. If all was subjective interpretation and constructed truth, rethinking something cannot improve accuracy, and I could never know if my beliefs were growing closer to reality. By contrast, in correspondence, if reality and my belief match, I know truth. All truth is neutral and the same from the viewpoint of other people or God. We all live in the same *uni*verse, the same reality, not a multiplicity of subjectively constructed ones.

I am not surprised postmodernism lends itself to presuppositional Reformed epistemology. While claiming to be based on an affirmation of depravity and grace, it actually takes significant postmodern influence. Romans 1 blames not the mind but the *will* for the suppression of truth. It quite literally says that all people can directly see the truth for themselves "in the things that have been made" or insofar as "that law is written on their hearts," that is, as their "conscience also bears witness" (Rom 1:20; 2:15). Jesus himself repeatedly points people to physical evidence in the form of his miracles. Paul and other apostles give many examples of and exhortations to reason with people in order to convert them.

Standing on One's Own Two Feet

Welbaum borrows many concepts from other systems without explaining how they still make sense in postmodernism while denying their foundation in realism. Examples include *essence, matter, mind-independent reality, being,* and *truth*. How can these concepts persist in a postmodernist system where reality and truth are a construct? Welbaum says, "the postmodernist is happy to join the classicalist" in many ways, but these agreements seem disconnected from the postmodern system. They are borrowed without justification and their defense and explanation is left to others. Meanwhile, Aristotelian Thomism and probably Gould's version of Christian Platonism propose comprehensive and biblical systems that stand on their own two feet.

In the end, I would like to see more clarity in the meanings of words, including comparisons with other systems. This is a widespread problem in postmodernism. Also, I would like to see postmodernism developed more as a metaphysic than an ethic. If it is not concerned with metaphysical questions, then I will stick with systems that provide answers.

4.4. IDEALISM RESPONSE—JAMES S. SPIEGEL

Introduction

At the outset of his chapter, Sam Welbaum states that his aim is "to justify the postmodern seat at this table, and indicate that its approach to metaphysics actually makes it in many ways more of an ally to Christianity than previously thought" (p. 104). Welbaum commences his discussion with some historical background which presumably is an indirect answer to the key question as to what metaphysics is. He says, "if one expects metaphysics to look as it did from Descartes through Hegel, then they would be hard pressed to find any metaphysical claims within postmodernism, aside from Heidegger's division between the ontic and the ontological" (p. 114). Welbaum adds that "some . . . presume that metaphysics is all but absent from postmodernity, when in reality it is a different set of fundamental questions that the postmodern metaphysician is asking" (p. 103).

Welbaum's historical precis distinguishes the classical, modern, and postmodern periods. He notes that metaphysics, or the search for ultimate truth about reality, dominated the classical period and that with the modern period, Descartes shifted the Western philosophical focus to epistemology and made certitude the standard for knowledge. Because of this impossibly high standard, the modernist project was destined to fail, thus paving the way for the postmodern response, which once again, especially through the work of Kierkegaard and Nietzsche, shifted the focus of philosophical concern, this time to issues of ethics and aesthetics. Welbaum observes, "Often postmodernity is seen as a rejection of absolute truth; in reality though, postmodernism is not overtly concerned with absolute truth or with objective reality" (p. 107).

Welbaum further expounds upon this point:

> while the modern philosopher might spend a fair amount of time attempting to prove that a chair exists, the postmodernist is happy to join the classicalist in simply sitting on the chair. That is by no means to say that the classicalist and the postmodernist agree on everything, but only that they both reject the modernist obsession with, and criteria for, certitude, and that makes postmodernity in many ways a swing back toward the classical. (p. 108)

There is a problem here. First, contrary to Welbaum's suggestion, the classicalist was not really content just to "sit in the chair." Classical philosophers such as Plato and Aristotle deeply engaged in metaphysical inquiry and speculation. Welbaum appears to ignore this when he proceeds to characterize postmodernism as a "swing back toward the classical." Although classicalists would join the postmodernist in eschewing the problematic modernist obsession with certitude, this similarity is dwarfed by the enormous divergence of the two approaches when it comes to systematic critical inquiry into the central metaphysical issues of the nature of substance, universals, the human soul, and God's relation to these things.

The principal difference between classicalism and modernism—as Welbaum's own historical analysis highlights—is epistemological in nature. It has nothing to do with difference of view on the importance and even basic methodology of metaphysical inquiry. Postmodernism is at odds with both classicalism and modernism—indeed, the entire sweep of Western philosophical history—on this score, except for the various skeptical camps that have cropped up at different points in philosophical history, from Pyrrhonism to Hume to Santayana.

As for the relationship between postmodernism and Christianity, Welbaum rightly acknowledges the tension between postmodernism and Christianity because of the postmodern emphasis on relativism and subjectivity. However, he goes on to note that postmodernism can be seen as an "ally to Christian thought" insofar as "we can conceive of postmodernism as a response to a secular, totalizing modernistic metanarrative, which inhabited Christian thinking in a negative way" (p. 110). Two problems here. First, one can reject the secularizing of metanarratives without repudiating the pursuit of metanarratives per se. There is a baby in that bathwater. Secondly, much of metaphysics has nothing to do with building "totalizing metanarratives" but rather focuses on specific issues regarding what lies beneath appearances (e.g., the nature of substance, persons, the human soul, etc.). Therefore, a serious pursuit of metaphysical inquiry is not really threatened by the adoption of the Lyotardian incredulity toward metanarratives.

Welbaum goes on to elucidate some key postmodern themes in twentieth-century philosophy: the Wittgensteinian (and perhaps Heideggerian) notion that language is inadequate to describe the world and the Kierkegaardian emphasis on subjective truth, leading to Welbaum's emphasis on subjectivity and the *experience* of the individual. This prompts Welbaum to conclude that

> the Christian postmodernist acknowledges her human frailty, her inability to know things beyond her scope, and the inherent subjectivity of her knowledge and of her world, but that does not mean that there is not an objective way that things actually are, toward which our subjectivity ought to point. For this reason, a Christian postmodern metaphysic is one that actually does not necessarily contradict other views (though it may), because while they are aiming at understanding the objective world as it is, the postmodernist is concerned with the subjective world as it is constructed. (p. 113)

To this I would offer a hearty "amen" when it comes to Welbaum's highlighting the limits of human understanding. However, it is also important to note that in making this claim about the world being subjectively constructed the postmodernist is making a *metaphysical* claim. In fact, it is essentially the same claim Kant made, as Welbaum goes on to acknowledge. The difference between Kant and the postmodernist, of course, is that at least Kant recognized he was doing metaphysics.

Welbaum says, "For Heidegger, and the postmodern thinkers who follow him, mankind's concern is not with the essence of a thing, but the *meaning* of a thing" (p. 115). The Heideggerian postmodernist may not be *concerned* with essences, but the question remains: Are essences real? If so, then acknowledge this and proceed with the practical applications and insights this understanding provides. If not, then concede the skeptical implications and practical ramifications this entails. This is more postmodern evasiveness—a refusal to seriously engage metaphysical questions without outright denying their significance and, as we will see below, without having to give up one's metaphysical commitments. This evasiveness is evident elsewhere, such as when Welbaum asserts that "a postmodern metaphysic is a study on the use of words, and the means of fostering and cultivating meaning, and care, as one interprets the world in which one lives" (p. 116). And yet, again, this is not truly a "metaphysic" but a refusal to do metaphysics in favor of a relativizing epistemology.

Like many Christian thinkers who want to embrace postmodernism, Welbaum is led headlong into incoherence. Consider two claims that he makes in the same paragraph toward the end of his chapter. On the one hand, Welbaum says [1]: "Postmodernism understands [metaphysical] questions to be ones of societal and individual construction" (p. 117). Yet just a few sentences later, he asserts [2]: "Christianity understands that God created all things, sustains all things, and moves sovereignly over all things" (p. 117). Because [2] is an assertion about God as sovereign creator and sustainer of all things, this necessarily involves metaphysical commitments, that is, beliefs about ultimate reality. But then how can this be squared with [1], the notion that all such metaphysical issues are mere social and individual constructions? These two claims are inconsistent. If so, then the notion of a "postmodern Christian" is an oxymoron. Welbaum goes on to say that Christians affirm God is creator of the cosmos and an omniscient being, having "complete objective knowledge of all things" (p.117). But again, these claims about God are metaphysical in nature. So a postmodern Christian would have to grant that they are mere "constructions" while at the same time affirm that they are absolutely true. How is this possible?

The incoherence of Welbaum's position is most evident in the final section where, in the context of addressing the case study of Peter and Paul, he affirms particular views on divine self-existence, the reality of a human essence, and personal persistence through time and into the afterlife. The metaphysical perspective Welbaum offers in this section is shallow and certainly not entailed by anything he has said previously, because in embracing postmodern foci on subjectivity and social construction he refuses to seriously engage in metaphysics. So is a truly Christian postmodern perspective actually just an excuse to avoid doing serious metaphysics? From where I stand, that would appear to be the case.

4.5 POSTMODERNISM REPLY—SAM WELBAUM

When we approach a topic, we bring with us quite a bit of baggage. Not only all of our background knowledge in other fields, but also any study, or preconceived ideas about the topic at hand. The essays in this book are no different. I greatly enjoyed reading my fellow author's responses to my essay, and look forward to addressing some of the concerns that they raised, but it is not my goal to untie everything that they may believe, or have asserted, about postmodernism, but rather to engage only where those beliefs intersect with my presentation. Space does not allow me to comment on everything, but so many of the questions and critiques point to the fundamental point I'm making that I believe I need to address them by functionally re-presenting my thoughts in a manner that hopefully allays at least a few concerns.

Initially though, I would like to address an elephant in the room. Postmodernism is not a Christian philosophy. Neither are Platonism, Aristotelianism, nor idealism. All four systems include, or may include, beliefs that do not line up with the teachings of Scripture, or that flat out contradict it. What any thinker does is take parts of a system that he or she finds appealing or useful and then massages them. This book includes Christianized versions of four schools of thought, but that also means that in that Christianizing, there are parts that get chipped away or are not present. The concern about trying to synthesize a framework and see how it works with Christian thought it not unique to the postmodern perspective, but this perspective is the most demonized, and least historically connected to Christian belief, so the issue seems more pronounced.

That said, Gould, Speigel, and Jacobs all take issue with the fact that it doesn't seem as though I'm doing metaphysics. Gould asserts that I haven't addressed the fundamental questions of metaphysics, Speigel asks if postmodern metaphysics is an excuse to avoid doing metaphysics, and Jacobs wonders if the whole discipline ought be called ethics and we should just move on. Fair questions all the way around. If the concerns and approaches of postmodern metaphysics are so drastically different, why not just call it something else?

I sympathize with the inclination, but the questions being addressed are metaphysical questions. What is real? What makes a thing a thing? What is the world? Does something persist over time? What is time? etc. The difference being where the questions are situated, and what answers are being sought. While the three other schools are asking the question in the ontic sphere, the postmodern is asking the question in the ontological sphere. None of us are going to deny the physical reality of objects. When I say that our worlds are constructed I'm not saying that in some way I project the physical matter of a chair into existence. The object is there. What I am saying is that the object exists in a field of other objects and each of those objects are in relation with one another, and in relation to me. When I address the chair, I'm addressing it as an object that I see in a matrix of relations. Further, what makes the chair a chair is a question related to how we approach the world, but postmodernism is far more concerned with what makes this chair this chair than what makes a chair in general a chair.

This point of focus is why Gould notes that postmodernism seems to have such a large tent. Postmodernism in no way denies the existence of an objective world, it denies the possibility of absolute certainty in my knowledge of the objective world, and it denies the possibility of an objective, non-situated, relation to the world. That, however, does not mean we cannot think about the objective world, that we cannot hypothesize about this world, in fact, that's what everyone does every single day. The postmodern emphasis though is that we do so from our situatedness. Yes, we can simply see the world, but when I see the red ball that Gould mentions, *I* am the one seeing the ball. My situatedness does not stop me from having direct access to the world, but there is a vast amount of disagreement about this thing toward which we have direct access. Any number of things might affect the way that I see that ball, however, I am the one seeing it, I am the one interpreting it, and I am the one projecting meaning on to it.

These last two statements send up red flags. What do we mean by interpreting and projecting meaning? One of the handicaps that postmodernism often faces in these discussions is we pick things like balls and chairs, which, in our mind, require no interpretation. They are just objects. This uncovers I believe another tendency that we see in discussing postmodernism, in this chapter it is most prominent in Jacobs' response, the inclination to presume that if everything is interpretation, then everyone is free to make up any fanciful thing that they can dream up. This is the case only in the hallowed halls of academia, the glitzy red carpets of Hollywood, and the rather bland screens of Tumblr and 4chan. The vast majority of interpretations are bland, normal, and merely an analysis of the essence, or the meaning of a thing.

Here though is the point. In my initial essay I said that postmodern metaphysics is more concerned with meaning than essence. Again, that does not mean that essence is contradictory to postmodern metaphysics, and however you want to analyze the world of physical matter, I am the one relating to it. In the front cover of one of my favorite books is a leaf. There is nothing special about the physical object. It is a plain leaf from a rather plain tree. The reason I have it though is that it was the first gift my then fifteen-month-old daughter gave to me, after deliberating for some time which one to hand me. The physical thing is a leaf, but it is a token of affection from one I care for deeply. It certainly is true that a wedding ring is just a piece of metal, but it also certainly is not the case that it is *just* a piece of metal.

Consider perhaps the experience of being at an estate sale. As you walk through the deceased's house, you see objects, some useful to you, some pretty, some you consider trash, and so on. What I am asserting is that the house that you are walking through was at one point a home. As humans we "home" the spaces that we inhabit and make places out of them. The deceased at one point moved into this house, this space, and it was foreign, cold, and distant from them. Over time they unpacked. They made the place theirs, and the house bears the marking of a home. As you looks at rings and necklaces, you search through date nights, weddings, and anniversaries. As you snicker at the bowling ball you snicker at every Tuesday night for over a decade. As you rifle through old clothes and toys, and pillows, you are pouring over the things that held meaning and import to these people. A ring is a ring, but it's more than a ring.

Certainly, that can all be dismissed as Hallmark movie sentimentalism, but my point is that it isn't. It may objectively be the case that your childhood home still exists, but the relations, the people, the time, all the factors that made that home your childhood home have ceased. The house stands, but the home is gone. The essence of that home is the relations that constructed it. Jacobs is correct, we all live in the same physical world, but Sire's book is aptly titled, the person next door lives in a different universe. That isn't solipsism. That isn't isolationist. Its merely the recognition that we are subjects, and that we project meaning onto objects. As I noted in my initial essay, Heidegger asserts that we are all homesick, and we are making a home out of this world.

To that point, the assertion that we shouldn't care about subjective interpretations of the world, that instead we ought to care about the world that God made, falls flat. There is no denial that there is a world. There is no denial that God made it a particular way. There is no denial that we can discuss it. However, be it Platonic, Aristotelian, idealistic, or any other number of ways of approaching that world, our manner of understanding it is part of the way that we conceive of the world, and construct the meaning of that world. Does that mean that I believe that we are trapped in our language, or trapped in our worldview? No, and I don't actually fully know what that would mean, and I would also venture neither do the other authors in this book. I remember saying it as a Masters student, but it never amounted to more than just being the type of thing a person is supposed to say about postmodernity. We are linguistic finite entities. We understand the world by the linguistic ways that we think about and interact with it. Is that to say that all knowledge is propositional, no of course not, but the ways that we understand the ontic world of physical objects is a building block off of which we construct the ontological world of meaning. Is it possible for a person to construct a world that does not line up with objective reality? Yes, it happens frequently, but that does not mean that it is not in fact the world in which they live.

In the dominant secularized understanding of postmodernity, this distinction is virtually non-existent. Foucault, Derrida, Rorty, and on down the line are not theistic thinkers. When they have no idea what the world in and of itself might objectively be, or what Heidegger's ontic world of matter is like, they also have no reason to think that we can approach that world, or that it even matters. However, that is descriptive of secular postmodernity, not prescriptive of postmodernity itself. When you insert the God of Christianity, what the postmodern approach to metaphysics does is allows the Christian thinker to better understand how the person they are addressing seems to be living in a different world. It also allows for a more fruitful understanding of meaning and purpose, which was eviscerated in modernity. Hence the Kierkegaardian call that one must find a truth that is true for them.

We come here to a point that I need to clarify that both Gould and Jacobs noted. I made the claim that there is one truth that is objectively true. This was an equivocation on my part in that I was using "truth" in what might be considered a "capital *T*" manner, as opposed to a "lower case *t*" manner. This distinction might be seen as empty in more analytic circles, but as used here, "truth" might be equated to facts, whereas "Truth" would be a life-orienting and existence-driving belief. Again, this is Kierkegaard's idea of holding to something with the passion of infinity. Or perhaps less theatrically, this is Augustine's assertion that faith requires assent, or James' noting that demons know the fact of God's existence and they shudder. In my initial essay I was unclear in that I made it sound as though the only thing factually accurate is the proposition "Christ exists." More plainly I meant that the only Truth is that Christ exists and the world is as He sees it. Our aim is for our subjectivity to come in line with Christ's objectivity.

I will leave it to the reader to determine if this is metaphysics or axiology (ethics/aesthetics). I personally approach the ontic world as a classicist, I tell my students I'm a postmodern-friendly Thomist. That means that I am aware that while I understand the ontic world to be such and such a way, that is part and parcel of the manner in which I conceive of and construct the world in my head. Postmodernism is wrong in many areas, but as a tool for understanding others, and understanding ourselves, it is a tremendous asset.

BIBLIOGRAPHY

Balthasar, Hans Urs von. *Love Alone Is Credible*. Translated by D. C. Schindler. San Francisco: Ignatius, 2004.
Boersma, Hans. *Heavenly Participation*. Grand Rapids: Eerdmans, 2011.
Drolet, Michael. *The Postmodernism Reader: Foundational Texts*. London: Routledge, 2004.
Derrida, Jacques. *Of Grammatology*. Translated by Gayatri Chakravorty Spivak. Baltimore: Johns Hopkins University Press, 2016.
Descartes, René. *Discourse On Method, and Meditations On First Philosophy*. 4th ed. Translated by Donald A. Cress. Indianapolis: Hackett, 1998.
Guinness, Os. *Dining with the Devil: The Megachurch Movement Flirts with Modernity*. Grand Rapids: Baker, 1993.
Heidegger, Martin. *The Fundamental Concepts of Metaphysics: World, Finitude, Solitude*. Bloomington, IN: Indiana University Press, 1995.
———. *The Metaphysical Foundations of Logic*. Translated by Michael Heim. Bloomington, IN: Indiana University Press, 1984.
———. *Ontology: The Hermeneutics of Facticity*. Bloomington, IN: Indiana University Press, 1999.
———. *The Question Concerning Technology, and Other Essays*. Translated by William Lovitt. New York: Harper Perennial, 2013.
Gregory, Stephan Brad. *The Unintended Reformation: How a Religious Revolution Secularized Society*. Cambridge, MA: Belknap, 2012.
Hume, David. *An Enquiry Concerning Human Understanding*. Oxford: Oxford University Press, 2007.
Kant, Immanuel. *Critique of Judgment*. New York: Oxford University Press, 2009.
Kierkegaard, Søren. *Concluding Unscientific Postscript to Philosophical Fragments*. Translated by Howard V. Hong and Edna H. Hong. Princeton, NJ: Princeton University Press, 1992.
———. *The Point of View*. Kierkegaard's Writings, Volume 22. Translated by Howard V. Hong and Edna H. Hong. Princeton, NJ: Princeton University Press, 1998.
Kimball, Dan. *The Emerging Church*. Grand Rapids: Zondervan, 2009.
Leff, Gordon. *The Dissolution of the Medieval Outlook*. New York: New York University Press, 1976.
Lyotard, Jean-François. *The Postmodern Condition: A Report On Knowledge*. Minneapolis: University of Minnesota Press, 1984.
McGrath, Alister E. *The Open Secret: A New Vision for Natural Theology*. Malden, MA: Blackwell, 2008.
Moreland, J. P., and Garrett DeWeese. "The Premature Report of Foundationalism's Demise." In *Reclaiming the Center*, edited by Millard J. Erickson, Paul Kjoss Helseth, and Justin Taylor, 81–108. Wheaton, IL: Crossway, 2004.
Nietzsche, Friedrich Wilhelm, and Walter Kaufmann. *The Portable Nietzsche: Selected and Translated, with an Introduction, Prefaces, and Notes*. Harmondsworth, UK: Penguin, 1976.

Nozick. Robert. "Philosophy and the Meaning of Life." In *Philosophical Explanations*, 571–610. Cambridge, MA: Harvard University Press, 1981.

Pascal, Blaise. *Pensées*. Translated by Roger Ariew. Indianapolis, IN: Hackett, 2005.

Reid, Thomas. "An Inquiry into the Human Mind." In *The Works of Thomas Reid*, Vol. 1, edited by William Hamilton. No loc: Elibron Classics, 2005.

Smith, James K. A. *Who's Afraid of Postmodernism? Taking Derrida, Lyotard, and Foucault to Church*. Grand Rapids: Baker Academic, 2006.

Webber, Robert. *Ancient-Future Worship*. Grand Rapids: Baker, 2008

Welbaum, Sam. "Defining Miracle: Hume, Theism and the History of a Concept." *Hope's Reason: A Journal of Apologetics* 3.1 (2013) n.p.

Willard, Dallas. "How Concepts Relate the Mind to Its Objects." *Philosophia Christi* 1.2 (1999) 5–20.

Index

absolutes, 110–11
abstract objects, 2–4, 10–13, 16, 19–10, 24–25, 27–29, 32, 59
abstracta, 4, 9, 21, 25
abstraction, 39–41, 47, 53 56, 61
accident(s), 17, 39, 43–44, 47
activism, 4, 9, 12, 16, 19, 32–33
actuality, 45, 67
aesthetics, 104–5, 107–8, 117, 130, 136
agent(s), 15, 30, 42, 58, 67, 79, 81
agnosticism, 83, 93
angels, 3, 44, 49, 51, 80
animals, 39, 43, 44–45, 48–49, 53, 80, 116
Anselm, 51 n.84, 66, 118
Aristotle, Aristotelian, Aristotelianism, x–xi, 3n9, 7–8, 10, 15–19, 25, 27–30, 35–68, 76–77, 87–88, 91–93, 98–99, 105n4, 125–26, 129–30, 133, 135
aseity, 3, 19, 51–52, 54–57, 64, 67
Augustine, Augustinian 22, 39, 66, 72, 108, 112, 118
Avicenna, 39, 41, 66
axiom of localization, 11, 20, 25

big-bang 9–10, 21, 23, 31
being, xii, 6n13, 8, 13–16, 22, 30–31, 35–39, 41, 44, 49n67, 51n80, 52, 54, 66–67, 71–73, 75, 80, 83, 107, 114, 114–15n26, 116, 119–21, 124, 126–27, 129
being-there, 120, 126–27
Berkeley, Berkeleyan, x, 42, 72–95, 97–100

Bible, xi, xii, 5, 43–44, 50, 55, 59, 66, 91, 93
bodies, body, bodily, x, 1, 15–16, 18, 21–23, 29–30, 37, 43–62, 65–68, 71, 72n1, 78, 82, 85–86, 90–91, 94, 94n. 47, 98, 119–20
body-soul, 10, 15, 18, 23, 30
Boethius, 39, 66
Bohr, Niels, 75
Boyle's Law, 84
brain, 46–49, 65, 91
bundle theory, 77–78, 90, 93

Cartesian dualism, 15, 17, 28
categories, 39, 64, 80, 98, 100
cause, 6, 13, 30, 38, 42, 43n37, 74n54, 51, 51n77,n80,n84, 53–54, 85, 92, 113
causation, 42, 49, 52, 98, 124123, 127
certainty, 106, 112–13, 122–23, 127–28, 134
change, 23, 36–38, 41–42, 50, 53–54, 57–58, 63, 65, 88, 94
Christ, 3, 14, 24, 52, 52n86, 66n105,n106, 109, 112, 123, 126–27, 136
Christianity, 17, 21, 24, 100, 104–5, 108–9, 114n26, 117, 121–22, 129–30, 132, 136
Clement, 66
concept(s), 2, 4, 6–7, 9, 12, 21, 23, 25, 31–32, 59, 61, 64, 72–73, 76, 87, 89, 99, 115, 120, 123, 127, 129
conceptualism, 76–77, 86
concrete, 9–13, 20–21, 24–26, 53, 56–57, 86–8

INDEX

concurrentism, 84–85, 90
consciousness, 72, 75, 81, 83, 92, 99, 125
continental philosophy, 103, 113, 125
creation *ex nihilo*, 63, 75, 89, 97
Cyril, 66

dasein, 114–16, 120
Davison, Andrew 31
Deleuze, Gilles, 95
Derrida, Jacques, 95, 104, 112–13, 116, 136
Descartes, Renee, 41, 45, 92–93, 103, 103n1, 105–6, 113, 118, 122, 129
divine simplicity, 51–52, 54–56, 66–67, 90
Dozel, James, 67
Drolet, Michael, 107
dualism, x-xi, 15, 17–18, 23, 28, 48, 50, 52–53, 60, 62, 65–66, 81n25, 82, 86, 90, 125

epistemology, 27, 41, 43, 47, 52n84, 60, 96, 100, 105, 105n4, 106–8, 118, 121, 125, 128–29, 132
essence(s), 17–18, 23, 38–39, 43–44, 50–55, 58, 60, 67, 79, 86, 110, 115, 117, 119–20, 124, 126–27, 129, 131–32, 134 135
Euclid, 43
exemplification, 11, 28, 76, 89
existence, ix-x, 6, 14–15, 17, 51, 54, 55, 67, 72n1, 75, 117, 136
existentialists, 107

fact(s), 11, 28n54, 29, 83, 89, 112, 123, 136
faith, 16–17, 28, 43,n35, 83, 94, 108, 110–12, 118, 136
form(s), 1, 2, 6n14, 10, 10n26, 17–18, 29–30, 36–45, 47–53, 57–60, 62–63, 65, 66n104, 76–78, 94
Foucault, Michel, 104, 113, 136

Geach, Peter, 126
genus, 43, 44n39
Gerson, Lloyd, 8, 27
Grossmann, Reinhardt, 11

Heidegger, Martin, 60, 104, 106, 109–11, 114–16, 119, 120n34, 122, 131, 135
Heraclitus, 21, 42n31
Hume, David, 17, 42n28, 61, 76n10, 109, 112–14, 116, 122, 130
hylomorphic, hylomorphism, 10n26, 23, 29–30, 38, 40, 45, 48–54, 58, 61, 64–66, 119, 125–27

idealism, ix-xi, 17, 25–26, 28, 42n28, 71–73, 75–78, 83–100, 128–29, 133
immaterialism, 72–73, 93, 96
individuals, 9, 16, 18, 27, 32, 40, 61, 63

Jesus, ix, xii, 18, 44, 46, 50, 52, 84, 94, 99, 109, 112, 123, 127, 128

Kant, Immanuel, 17, 42n28, 64, 72, 92, 93n44, 94n48, 106, 111, 114, 116, 118, 131
Kierkegaard, Soren, 103, 106, 111–12, 119, 122, 130
knowledge, 18, 35, 40–42, 44–45, 47, 49, 53, 59, 64–65, 81–82, 92, 104–7, 111, 113, 117, 123, 128–29, 131–32, 134–35

language, xi, 78–80, 93, 95, 104, 110–11, 113, 118, 122–23, 126–27, 131, 135
Locke, John, 73, 77, 93, 95,
logic, 6, 41, 42, 64
Lyotard, Jean Francois, 103n1, 107, 113

materialism, x-xii, 2n3, 28, 37, 40, 48, 92, 96
matter, 10n24, 15–16, 30, 36–38, 42, 45, 47, 50, 51n75, 53, 57–60, 62–63, 65, 73–74, 83, 86n37, 87, 94, 96, 100, 114–15, 124, 126, 129, 134, 136
Menzel, Christopher, 4, 19,
mind, 10, 12, 17, 19, 25, 39–41, 45–46, 48, 63–66, 74–84, 86–93, 96–98, 100, 114, 118, 128

mind of God, x, 20, 4, 59, 76–77, 86, 118
mind-body, 18, 45, 81–82, 86
mind-dependent, 72, 74–75, 77, 83, 86–89, 97, 100
mind-independent, 12, 13,n34, 76, 82, 87–88, 92, 100, 123, 126, 129
monism, x–xi, 83, 96, 100
Moreland, J. P., xii, 57
Morris, Thomas, 4–5, 19
Muller, Richard, 67

naturalism, 63, 87
Nietzsche, Friedrich, 106, 112, 113, 126, 130
nominalism, nominalist(s), xi, 2, 11, 29, 40, 53, 61, 63, 76–77, 122

objective reality, 107, 113, 118, 119–20, 123, 130, 135
occasionalism, occasionalist, 84–85, 98
Ockham's razor, 73, 83, 92, 96, 100
ontological, ontologies, ontology, ix, xi–xii, 3, 9, 11–12, 14–15, 19, 26, 29, 51n84, 52, 59, 67, 76, 80, 81, 83, 89, 98, 103, 105n4, 106, 113–16, 124, 126, 129, 133, 135

panentheism, 3, 22, 89, 97
pantheism, pantheistic, 3, 22, 51n80, 93, 96, 100
participation, 8–9, 14, 21, 22, 30–31
particular(s), 11, 13, 14, 20, 22, 25, 49, 50, 57, 61, 63–65, 71, 76–79, 81, 86
Pascal, Blaise, 106, 112, 118
perception(s), x, 60, 72n1, 83n32, 88, 92–95, 99, 128
person(s), xi, 14, 17–18, 29–30, 36, 45–48, 50, 52, 57, 59–60, 66, 93–94, 112, 114n26, 116, 126, 131, 135
personal identity, 15, 23, 71, 82
phantasm(s), 46–47, 49
phenomenological, phenomenology, xi, 17, 28, 103–4, 113
physics, xi, 36n4, 38, 42–43, 72, 74, 84, 92, 100

Plantinga, Alvin, 4
Plato, 2n3, 6n14, 8, 17–19, 22, 27, 29, 38–41, 45, 59, 66n106, 72, 76, 87, 105n4, 115, 130
Popper, Karl, 74
Porphyry, 43
predicate(s), 11, 36–37, 39, 62–63, 65, 89, 92–93
predication(s), 55, 66, 89, 90
presuppositionalism, 17, 28, 94
properties, property, 4, 9–12, 14–15, 17, 19–20, 23–30, 32, 40, 43–44, 53–57, 61, 63–67, 71, 75–78, 86, 87–90, 115, 124, 138
proposition(s), 4, 9, 12–13, 31, 39–40, 55, 62–63, 110–11, 126

qualities, quality, 10–11, 36, 37n8, 39, 43–44, 72n1, 73–74, 76, 78–79, 86–91, 93–95, 98–99
Quine, W. V. O, 7, 10n10

realism, x–xii, 16, 24–25, 28n54, 29, 40, 56–57, 76–77, 92, 94n48, 122, 127, 129
relations, 4, 9, 17, 19, 32, 52, 55
relativism, 28, 93, 104, 112, 122, 130
resurrection, i, x, 15, 18, 30, 50, 53, 57, 62, 66, 86, 94, 99, 119–20

science, 5, 68, 72, 74, 84, 88, 100, 106
situatedness, 60–61, 116, 123, 134
skepticism, 83, 88, 93–94, 99, 105, 107, 116, 126–12
solipsism, 93, 99, 135
soul, ix–x, xii, 15–16, 18, 22–23, 29–30, 37n8, 40, 44–45, 48–50, 52–3, 57–60, 62
spirit, 65–66, 68, 71, 78, 80, 82, 86, 90–91, 94, 98, 119, 125, 119, 127, 130–31
substance(s), x, 4, 9–11, 13–19, 22–23, 27–30, 36, 38–39, 42–45, 50, 52–55, 58–60, 63, 65–67, 71, 73, 78, 80, 82–83, 86–87, 89–90, 92–93, 95–98, 113, 117, 124, 127, 130–31
substrata, substrate, substratum, 37, 59, 73–74, 77–78, 87, 93–95, 99

teleological(ly), teleology, 10, 90, 98, 126
theism, xiii, 2n3, 57, 83
theology, 2n2, 5n13, 42–43, 51n83, 67, 72, 108, 111, 120, 122
Thomas Aquinas, x, 3, 15n38,n41, 16–18, 29, 35–55, 60, 64–67, 92, 93n44,n46
thought(s), 9, 12–13, 56,n95, 92–93,
top-downism, 8, 27–28
transcendentals, 39, 52
trope(s), 11, 56
truth, 5, 41n27, 42, 43n35, 52, 56, 59, 64, 105–7, 110–12, 119, 122–23, 126–30, 136
truthbearers 55–56

universal(s), ix-xii, 2–3, 1113, 16–18, 20, 25, 27–29, 38–40, 43–44, 47–49, 51n80, 53, 56–59, 61, 63–66, 71, 75–80, 86, 89, 94, 117, 119–20, 125–27

van Inwagen, Peter 3, 91

whole(s), 3, 8, 10, 14, 16, 18, 24, 30, 45, 48, 52, 57, 59, 65–66, 90
Willard, Dallas, xii
Wippel, John, 68
Wittgenstein, Ludwig, 42n28, 93n44, 110, 113, 126
Wolterstorff, Nicholas, 3, 67, 96
word(s), 12 78–79, 110, 116, 126–27, 129, 132
worldview, 73, 128, 135

Yandell, Kieth, 3

www.ingramcontent.com/pod-product-compliance
Lightning Source LLC
Chambersburg PA
CBHW022124160426
43197CB00009B/1151